The *Stretch&Sew* Pants Book

The *Stretch&Sew* Pants Book

By Ann Person

Published by Stretch & Sew, Inc.
Eugene, Oregon

Contents

Introduction

Easy to sew, fast, simple, and comfortable. These are all words that describe Stretch and Sew Slacks and Shorts Pattern 700. A pull-on pant that has been the heart of our business for over seven years, over 2-million copies of this popular pattern have been sold. It is a wardrobe basic for women all over the United States and Canada.

In addition to pull-on pants, we have developed a Jeans Pattern 710 for women. Pattern 3700, designed like Pattern 700, is available for the queen size woman.

Pants have become a way of life in today's society. And, when you combine knits and pants, you have a garment that will add style and comfort to every wardrobe.

Moreover, changing fashions will inspire you to sew up-to-the-minute styles. This book provides you with all the information you will need to follow fashion trends as well as to insure a flattering fit.

Like all Stretch and Sew patterns, our Slacks and Shorts Pattern is printed in a range of sizes on a master pattern. This enables the home seamstress to sew not only for herself but for others as well. And, to combine sizes for a better fit on one individual.

Both the sewing instructions included with the pattern and Chapter Two in *The Stretch & Sew Sewing Book* offer a guide to basic fit and construction. This publication is intended to give you supplementary information with tips on fabric selection, fitting, and alterations, as well as easy-to-do design changes.

1

Fabric for Your Pants

Fabric for Your Pants

Selecting the proper fabric for your pants is important. Knowing what to look for regarding the stretch, the memory, and other properties of the fabric will increase the satisfaction you will feel when you finish a new garment.

FABRIC MEMORY

Check for fabric memory by stretching a portion of the fabric at least 10 inches in from the cut edge. If the fabric returns to its original shape, it has good memory. Your pants will sew together well and retain their shape during wearing.

STRETCH OF FABRIC

The Stretch and Sew Slacks and Shorts Pattern 700 is designed for use with a fabric with 25 per cent stretch. The stretch in the fabric becomes ease in the garment.

The method for determining the percentage of stretch is simple. Fold your fabric at least 10 inches from one cut edge. Take 10 inches of the fabric on the fold and stretch. If it will stretch easily to 12-1/2 inches, you have 25 per cent stretch. If it stretches to only 11 inches, you have less than 25 per cent stretch. If, when you take 10 inches of fabric, it stretches to 15 inches, you have 50 per cent stretch. (Fig. 1)

An important question is, "Will it stretch *easily*?" Don't stretch with all your might. If I can stretch a piece of fabric easily to show 25 per cent stretch, I can usually force it to show 35 per cent stretch.

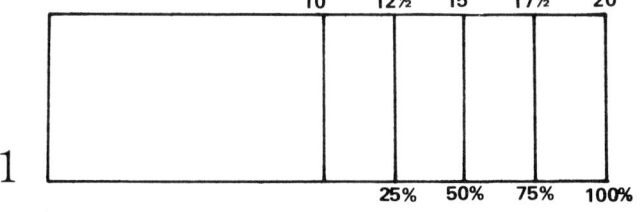

1

As the stretch of the fabric increases, the size pattern you should use decreases. If your measurements indicate that you should use a size 36, you would use that size for fabric with 25 per cent stretch. If the fabric has 50 per cent stretch, your pattern should be size 34. The reverse would be true for a fabric with less stretch. In this case, a twill that has 12-1/2 per cent stretch would require a pattern halfway between size 36 and size 38.

These are easy principles to remember and they will help you in properly fitting your garment.

CREASING PROPERTIES OF FABRIC

Fabric with a fine gauge—fine yarn in a closely knit pattern—will crease most easily. Many men's wear fabrics have this property. Women's wear fabrics often have a greater amount of bulk to create surface interest. These fabrics make beautiful pants. But you must remember that it is more difficult to put a sharp crease in bulky or more loosely knit fabric.

The effect you wish to create will determine your choice. A very tailored and crisp look can be achieved from a fine men's wear fabric. The crease is often de-emphasized in a couture design.

It seldom will be necessary to topstitch a polyester on the crease line. Even with a heavy Jacquard, the crease may be pressed in with a damp cloth and your iron set for wool. Always protect a synthetic with a press cloth. Topstitching is usually necessary for a nylon or cotton double knit where the crease is difficult to heat set.

NAPS, PATTERNS, AND PLAIDS

Most knit fabrics do have a nap. It is always best to position your pattern pieces so the garment will be cut with the nap of the fabric going the same direction. There are exceptions but they are rare, and I have found it safe to follow this rule: If you feel you can save a great deal of fabric by reversing the pattern pieces, a good test will be to sew two pieces of the fabric together which have been cut from opposite directions. Take the piece to the light and try to see if there is a variation in shading. (Fig. 2) If the effect is pleasing, it will no doubt be safe to cut the garment in the same fashion.

2

Fabric with a pattern or design also needs to be studied before cutting. There is often a direction to the design which may go unnoticed until the garment is completed. Always unfold your fabric and look at the design to determine the best direction for cutting.

Plaids present an extra design dimension. When selecting a plaid for pants, keep in mind the size of the person for whom you are sewing. The plaid should be flattering but not overwhelming. The extra time it takes to match plaids will provide a garment much more satisfying to wear. For additional interest, cut your pants fabric on the bias. A completely new look can be achieved by the creative use of fabric.

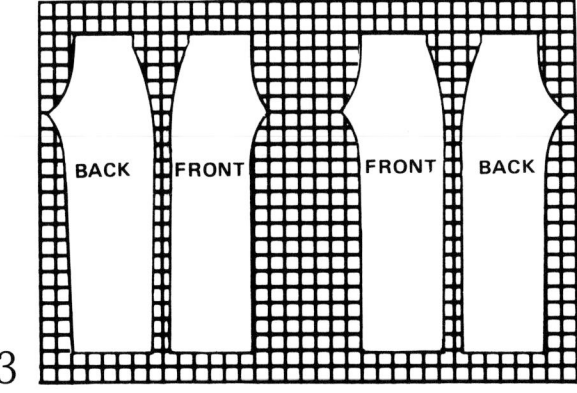

3

To match a plaid or any other fabric with a dominant pattern, follow the layout. (Fig. 3) Always match from seamline to seamline rather than from cut edge to cut edge. One thickness of fabric should be cut at a time. Start with the fronts, exactly matching one to another. Then, match the side seams of the backs to the side seams of the fronts. You will be delighted with the results.

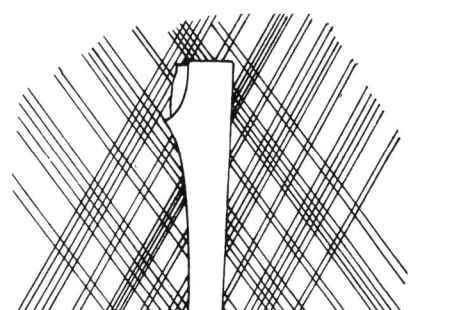

4

To match a bias plaid, fold each pattern piece in half, lengthwise. Place a pattern piece on the fabric with the fold running through the intersections of the diamonds. (Fig. 4) This will insure that the design is balanced in your garment. Unfold the pattern piece and pin it to the fabric. Repeat this process for each piece.

If you have chosen an uneven plaid or a diagonal plaid that seems impossible to match exactly, eliminate the outside leg seam on your pants. Directions for this technique are found in Chapter Five.

PRE-CARE OF FABRIC

One of the great advantages of sewing your own garments is that you are able to pre-treat the fabric—either wash and dry or steam it—before you cut and sew. In a factory where production is vital, this special treatment of the fabric is not possible. You have the advantage in this case and will be assured of many wonderful days of wear and pleasure from your garment. A few extra minutes here will prevent disappointment later.

Fabric must be prepared before it is cut. The rule for sewing with knit fabric is: Treat your fabric before it is cut exactly as it is going to be treated after it has been sewn into a garment. Most knits will shrink as much as 3 per cent. Let this happen to your fabric before you cut it.

Use a mild soap or detergent for the first washing since soap will remove any excess dye that could be in the fabric. Do not mix new dark-colored fabric with light-colored fabrics because synthetics have a tendency to pick up dye. If you plan to dry clean a wool knit garment, take the fabric to the dry cleaner and ask him to steam the piece before you cut it.

Synthetic fabrics, such as polyester, should be washed in a mild water temperature. Dryers are permissible if the cycle is short and the temperature is cool. Hot water and hot dryers can cause permanent creases and wrinkles in polyesters, nylons, and all synthetic fabrics that require heat setting in their finishing process. The wash-and-wear characteristics of most synthetics are fantastic but treat them gently so your garments will stay lovely for a long time.

FABRIC FIBERS

Cotton is a natural fiber. Since cotton often shrinks more than synthetics, be certain to pre-shrink it. Cotton double knit for pants cannot be beat for comfort on a summer day. If you live in a hot, humid climate, you will appreciate this wonderful fabric. Cotton launders beautifully in warm water and may be dried in a dryer. Hot water will cause more shrinkage than cool water. Creases, if desired, should be stitched in by machine.

Wool is a natural fiber with an elegant look. Warm and comfortable, it holds a crease, resists wrinkles, and tailors handsomely. Wool should be dry cleaned.

Polyester is a synthetic fiber and is excellent for women's pants. It is wrinkle-resistant, washes beautifully, and holds a crease without stitching. It should be laundered with a light load in warm water on a perma-press cycle and dried in a cool dryer. Touch-up pressing is usually unnecessary.

Acrylic is a wonderful synthetic fiber. Because of its wool-like appearance, it is often used in place of wool for children's clothes, which must be laundered frequently. Garments of acrylic should be turned inside out and laundered with a light load in cool or warm water. The gentle cycle is best. The fabric may be dried in a cool dryer or laid out to dry. Do not hang the fabric or the finished garment to drip dry. With a little special care, an acrylic garment will retain its beauty for many, many wearings.

Nylon is a synthetic fiber that is very strong, has good stretch, and is easily laundered. If a sharp crease is desired, it can be stitched in. Pant weight nylon is especially good for children's pants because it is so durable.

Blends of fibers are often used for women's pants. Common blends are cotton and polyester, cotton and acrylic, polyester and acrylic, polyester and silk, polyester and linen, nylon and acetate, and cotton and rayon. When fibers are combined, the fabric usually takes on some of the characteristics of each. For example, when a natural fiber is combined with a synthetic fiber, the natural fiber will give the fabric better breathing properties and it will be more comfortable to wear.

Remember, as the seamstress, you are also the designer. Fabric choice will determine your finished garment's look. A fabric with a firm hand will produce a crisp, tailored look in a pair of pants. A softer fabric lends itself to a wider leg because it drapes nicely. Care taken in fabric selection will reap dividends for you in providing the look you want. Remember, also, to handle your knits with tender loving care. You'll be delighted with the results.

2

Measuring and Fitting

Measuring and Fitting

To sew a pair of pants that will fit perfectly, you will need Stretch and Sew Slacks and Shorts Pattern 700. Use dotted *Perky* Pattern Paper to prevent errors in drafting and pattern adjustments.

Take your measurements and read the tape carefully and accurately. I have two measurements for my hips and waist: One that is actual and one that I think would be nice. But a little white lie here can cause many unhappy moments when you are doing your final fitting. So measure carefully and follow the measurements.

The measurements on your Stretch and Sew pants pattern are the exact body measurements that were used to grade the pattern in the various sizes. A wonderful thing about Stretch and Sew patterns is that the waist and hip have been graded in 2-inch increments. This enables you to make size adjustments very easily.

If your waist measures 2 inches smaller than the waist measurement for your hip size, simply grade down one full size at the waist. If, instead of a full size, your waist measures 1 inch smaller (or one-half size smaller than the pattern measurement), simply grade your pattern halfway between the two size divisions. The reverse is true if the waist must be enlarged. I have found it best to fit my pants by my hip measurement and make any necessary adjustments at the waistline.

HIP MEASUREMENT

Accurate measurements are a must. To determine the proper size to trace from your master pattern, take a hip measurement 7 inches down from the waist over undergarments to be worn with pants. The pattern was designed for the hip measurement to be taken at this point even though women measure larger at the 9-inch drop from the waist. The pants pattern is proportionately larger at the 9-inch drop, but the 7-inch measurement is the one that is used in determining your size. (Fig. 1)

If the proper size is selected, your pants will hang freely from the hips in a smooth and flattering line. If you use too small a size, your pants will stretch over your hips and creases will occur in the crotch and upper leg. This tends to accentuate any bulges or indentations that we would prefer to have passed unnoticed.

WAIST MEASUREMENT

A waist measurement should be taken next. Measure firmly but not too tightly. (Fig. 2) The waist of the pants is finished with elastic and the proper length of elastic is your exact waist measurement minus 1 inch.

If your measurements do not fit those on the pattern, you should add or subtract where necessary. For example, if your hip measures 40 inches and your waist measures 33 inches, you should increase the waist size of the pattern. This is accomplished by adding to the side seams on both

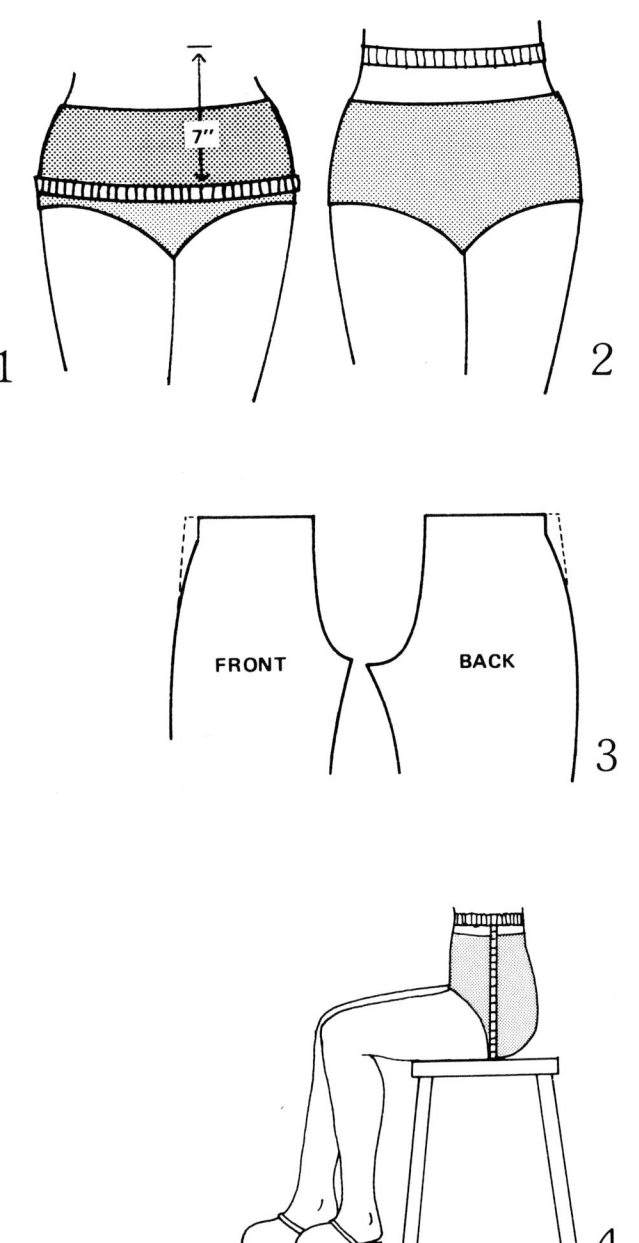

the front and back pattern pieces. (Fig. 3) The proper ease will remain in the waist if you follow this procedure. And it will result in a smoother and more comfortable fit over the tummy.

You also may use a smaller waist size if the fabric will allow. Remember that the fabric and elastic must pull up over the hips. If this adjustment is necessary, it would be wise to use a fabric with at least 30 to 50 per cent stretch. Check your fabric stretch carefully before making this alteration in your pattern.

CROTCH DEPTH

Probably the most important measurement of all is the *crotch depth* or *sit measurement*. Women so often sew pants that fit in the hips and waist but pull in the crotch because they aren't long enough. Or the pants are terribly baggy because they are too long in the crotch.

Take the crotch depth measurement by tying a piece of elastic around your waist. Sit on a flat surface with your feet on the floor and measure from the lower edge of the elastic to the surface of the chair. (Fig. 4) It is easy to get an incorrect measurement if you don't sit up straight. If you lean over to see what the measurement is, you completely distort the true picture. So, sit up straight! Only accurate measurements will produce good-fitting pants.

Your Stretch and Sew Slacks and Shorts Pattern has a chart which gives the allowed sit measurement for each size. Check your measurement with the one for your size on the pattern instruction sheet. If your measurement matches exactly, no adjustment is necessary. However, if it differs, go to your pattern for a quick but necessary alteration.

A line has been drawn on both the pattern front and pattern back labeled *shorten or lengthen here for crotch depth.* This is where the adjustment is made.

To shorten the crotch depth, cut on the line for shortening or lengthening and lap the amount of difference between your measurement and that on the chart. (Fig. 5) <u>This must be done equally on the front and back pattern pieces.</u> Use your fashion ruler to even out the crotch line.

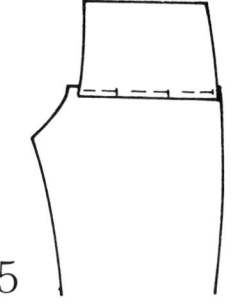

5

To lengthen the crotch depth, reverse the procedure. Cut the pattern front and pattern back on the line for shortening or lengthening and add extra pattern paper to make the pattern crotch depth and the body crotch depth measurement the same. (Fig. 6)

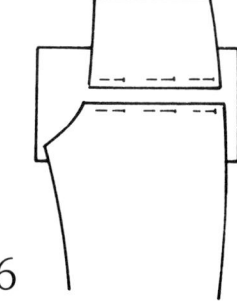

6

It is always good to keep in mind that the back and front pieces are going to be sewn together into one garment. So they must be equal in length. More length in one seam or another will cause a twisting of the pant leg. This is a common error in adjusting the Slacks and Shorts Pattern for crotch depth. That is why the dotted paper is a must when you draft your initial pattern. By lining up the center grain line with the vertical dots on the paper, you will keep everything plum and square. Don't forget! The changes you make in the front should be made in the back to keep the front and back the same length.

PANT LENGTH

You will want to measure for a finished pant length. This should be determined while drafting your initial pattern. Measure from the waistline over the curve of the hip or straight down the front to the ankle or to the length you prefer for your pants. Add the 1-1/2 inch hem allowance to this measurement.

It is helpful to write on the pattern your finished length for slacks as well as shorts. This will save you time whenever you sew a pair of pants. I also like to note the fabric and date so that after a period of time my memory will be refreshed as to how I liked a certain pant length. It also makes it easy to recall pants of a specified fabric and remember if the length noted is appropriate for the new pair, keeping in mind leg style, shoe heel, and so on. An adjustment in length can be made more simply when this is noted on the pattern.

You are well on your way to having a pattern for pants that will fit your figure. What an accomplishment! For many women, these simple measurements will be sufficient. If, after trying on your pants, you have some extra wrinkles, pulls, or creases, please go to Chapter Three, "Special Fitting Problems," for additional information about specific figure types and ways to deal with each.

3

Special Fitting Problems

Special Fitting Problems

Your figure type will dictate the alterations that will have to be made to the pattern to achieve a perfect fit. If your body is nearly in accordance with standard measurements, you will be able to select the proper size and cut and sew a pair of pants in a matter of minutes. But, if you do not fit the measurement chart or if you have variances in your figure type that have inspired you to sew your own pants, then you will have to devote some time to the basic information we have prepared for you in this chapter.

Here again you will find it necessary to be very observing of your own figure and you will also find it necessary to pay very close attention to detail. A little bulge will call for a little extra fabric to accommodate the bulge.

I have a favorite saying I use when I am talking to women about pattern fitting and adjustments: "Do what you think needs to be done. Add the fabric where the body needs it. If you need extra room in the tummy, allow for it in your pattern. If your hips are full in the lower part of your derriere, add fullness to accommodate. Don't be afraid to try anything that seems possible. Whatever you add, you can take away later if you find it necessary."

Before you consider these things, remember that pants fitting too tightly will have many creases and wrinkles. Be certain the pants fall freely over the hip and the fabric is not stretched around the body. Whenever a knit is stretched snugly over the body, creases will occur. Horizon-tal creases will shorten and accentuate heaviness in the leg and hip, but free-falling pants will create an illusion of slimness that can never be created by a pair of pants that look as if the woman has been poured in. The only way to correct this is to make a larger size.

Your problem could result from taking inaccurate basic measurements. For instance, a crotch that is too short will account for a smile in the front of a pair of pants. The crotch depth must be sufficient so that the fabric does not touch the body. A good test is to measure from the center front through the crotch to the center back. Compare this to the curve on your pattern pieces, measuring on the seamline. Double check your other basic measurements before trying additional alterations.

Also, please remember that the Stretch and Sew Slacks and Shorts Pattern has an excellent curve in the crotch which should not be tampered with. (Fig. 1) If the crotch depth is adjusted at the line for shortening and lengthening on the pattern, it must be done exactly the same front and back. Length may be added or removed from the crotch shelf by making adjustments at the inside leg seam. This procedure is described in the section beginning on the next page.

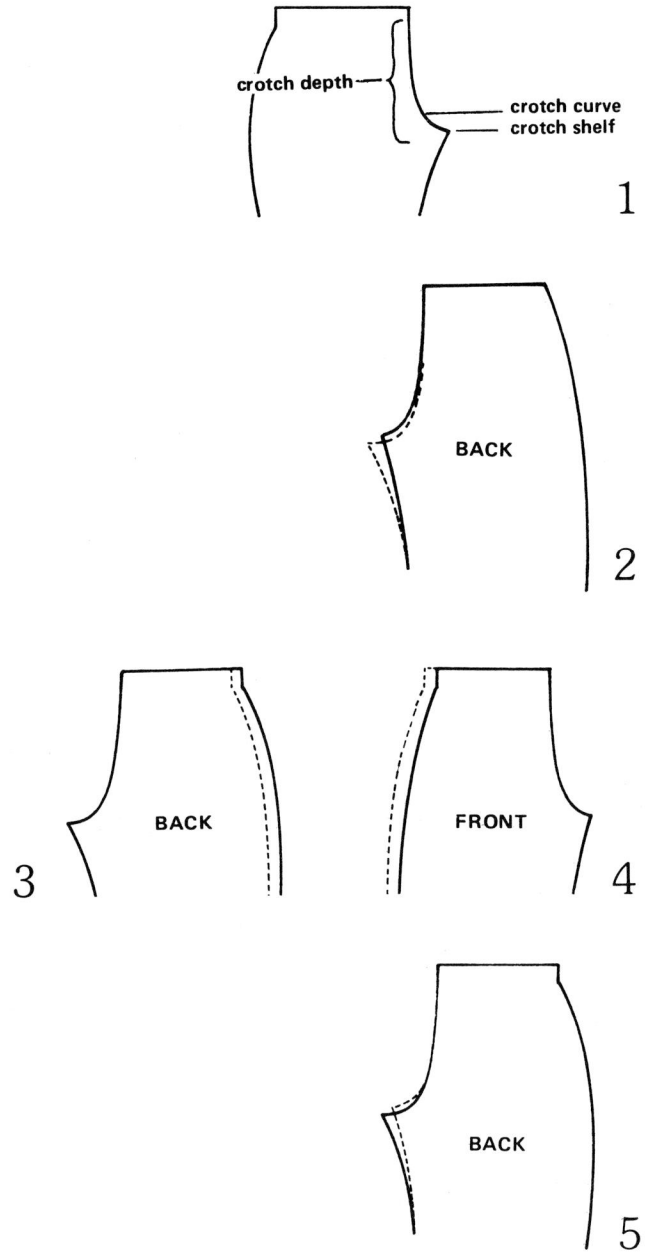

LARGE DERRIERE

For a proportionately large derriere, the shelf in the pants crotch is often too short. There is not sufficient curve in the back to allow the pants to cover the seat without creating a pull underneath or pulling the whole garment down from the waist. This tightness may also cause a twisting of the pants creases.

To correct this, the shelf must be lengthened at the inside leg seam on the back only. (Fig. 2) When the shelf is lengthened, the inside leg seam is also lengthened. To compensate for this added length, drop the shelf in the back slightly. (Fig. 2) Make certain the front and back inside leg seams are identical in length. If they are not, a twist in the crease or seam will be readily apparent.

FLAT DERRIERE

For a flat derriere, you may find that by scaling down the outside leg seam on the back one full size, you will achieve a better fit. (Fig. 3) It is possible to use, for example, a size 34 back and a size 36 front. If the tummy is proportionately much larger than the derriere, the fabric removed from the side seam in the back may be added to the front. (Fig. 4)

If the back crotch shelf is too long, there will be extra fabric under the seat and it will be necessary to shorten the shelf to remove this fabric. (Fig. 5) When shortening the shelf, you also shorten the back inside leg seam so it is necessary to raise this seam slightly (Fig. 5) to keep it the same length as the front inside leg seam. If the pants already have been cut, you may shorten the shelf and then shorten the front inside leg seam at the bottom to match the back inside leg seam. Make adjustments on your pattern for a future pair.

FLAT DERRIERE   LARGE DERRIERE

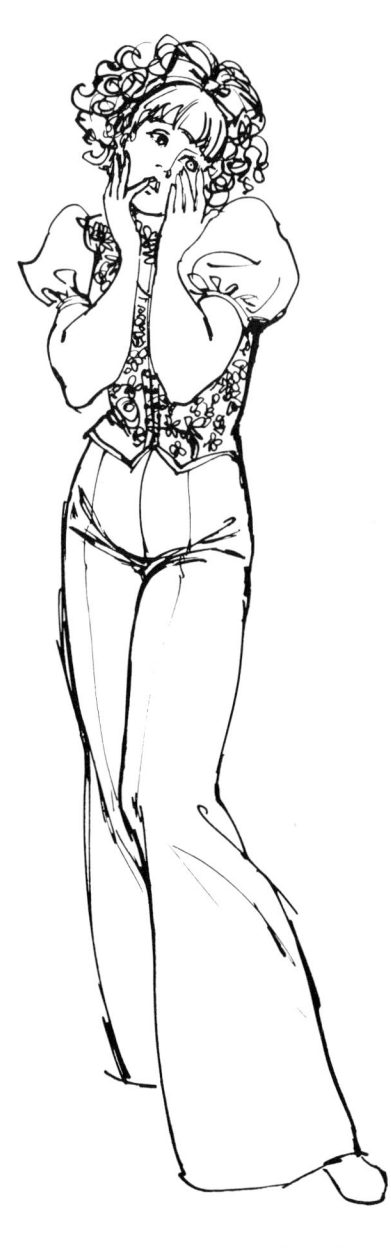

LARGE TUMMY

FLAT TUMMY

LARGE DERRIERE
AND LARGE TUMMY

LARGE TUMMY

For a large tummy, the shelf in the crotch is often too short. There is insufficient curve in the front to allow the pants to cover the tummy without creating a pull underneath or a pulling down of the whole garment from the waist. Tightness may also cause a twisting of the pants creases. To correct this, the shelf on the front pattern piece must be lengthened at the inside leg seam. (Fig. 6) When the shelf is lengthened, the inside leg seam is also lengthened. Slightly dropping the shelf in the front, as illustrated, will bring the front inside leg seam back to the same length as the back inside leg seam.

FLAT TUMMY

If you are a woman with a flat tummy, you may find that you will need to scale down the front seams of your pants one full size. For example, you may use a size 34 hip for the front and a size 36 hip for the back. (Fig. 7) Keep the inside leg seam length and the crotch depth the same on both front and back. If your derriere happens to be proportionately much larger, you may need to add to the back side seam the amount that you removed from the front. (Fig. 8)

LARGE DERRIERE AND LARGE TUMMY

If you have a rounder than average figure, you will probably need an extended crotch shelf in both the front and the back to relieve tightness and to prevent the creases from twisting. (Fig. 9) A greater amount will usually be added to the back inside leg seam as illustrated.

Remember with this adjustment, the inside leg seams, front and back, must be identical in length when stitched. It might be necessary to raise or lower the crotch shelf a slight amount to keep these seams the same length.

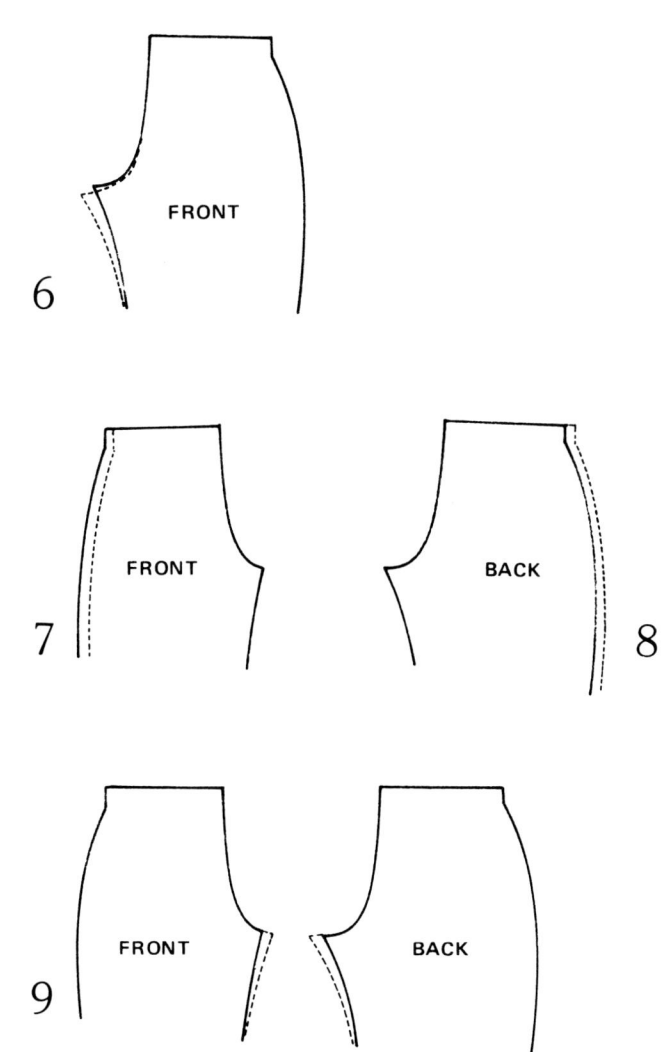

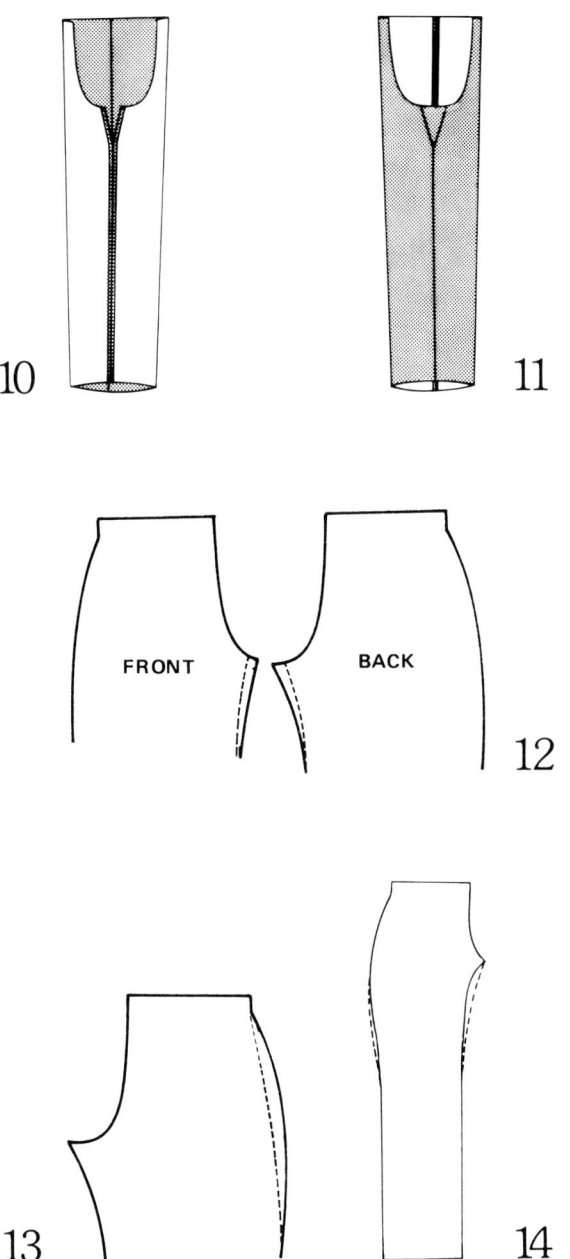

FRONT   BACK

10 11 12 13 14

If the pants have been sewn and you find the shelf was really not wide enough for a proper fit, open the inside leg seam (Fig. 10), and add a wedge to compensate. (Fig. 11) This adjustment will be only slightly visible when made of identical fabric and can add a great deal to comfort and fit.

FLAT DERRIERE AND FLAT TUMMY

If you find on observation that you have a flat derriere and a flat tummy, the crotch shelf can be narrowed on both the front and the back inside leg seams. (Fig. 12) The greater amount would usually come from the back inside leg seam as illustrated.

Remember with this adjustment that the inside leg seams, front and back, must be identical in length when stitched. It might be necessary to raise or lower the shelf a slight amount on the front or back to keep these seams even.

FLAT SIDE HIP

The curve at the hip on Pattern 700 allows for an average roundness in a figure. If, in looking at your figure, you see a straighter-than-average hip line, you may want to straighten out your side seam at the hip, following the illustration. (Fig. 13) This will remove unnecessary fullness and prevent your pant creases from swinging in.

HEAVY UPPER THIGH

The legs of your pants should hang freely from your hips to be most flattering, especially if your upper thigh is heavy in proportion to your hip size. More room can be achieved in the upper leg by adding slightly to both the inside and outside leg seams at the thigh. This must be done gradually if you are to have a nice line. (Fig. 14)

FLAT DERRIERE
AND FLAT TUMMY

FLAT SIDE HIP

HEAVY UPPER THIGH

SLIM UPPER THIGH LONG BACK SHORT BACK SWAYBACK

SLIM UPPER THIGH

When the upper thigh is slim in proportion to the hip size, unwanted fullness often occurs in the upper leg. The extra fullness should be removed equally from the front and back inside leg seams. (Fig. 15) However, this adjustment will shorten the crotch shelf. If the fabric is needed through the shelf, a slight curve can be made on the inside leg seam itself, removing extra fullness. (Fig. 16) Be careful not to make this curve too abrupt or other pull lines will occur. A slight degree of change can make a big difference.

LONG BACK

If your back is longer than average or if you are full through the lower back, it will be necessary to add extra length to your pattern. Extend the center back seam and taper it to the side seam. (Fig. 17)

SHORT BACK

If your back is shorter than average or if you are especially flat through the lower back, it will be necessary to shorten the center back seam on your pattern. Shorten the center back seam and taper it to the side seam. (Fig. 18)

SWAYBACK

Even a slight swayback can cause a roll of fabric just under the waist elastic in the back of the pants. It would appear that trimming this extra fabric away would solve the problem. It does, until you sit down. Then, the pants pull down and there is an uncomfortable gap. The correct way to remove this extra fabric in pants is to take a deeper seam at the top 3 to 4 inches of the center back seam. (Fig. 19) This removes the roll of excess fabric, but the pants stay put whether you're standing or sitting.

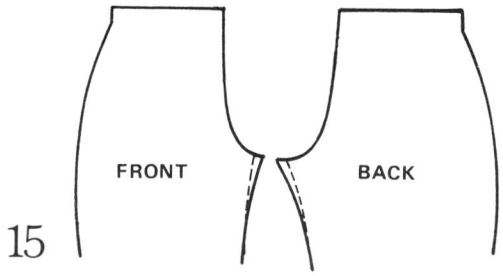

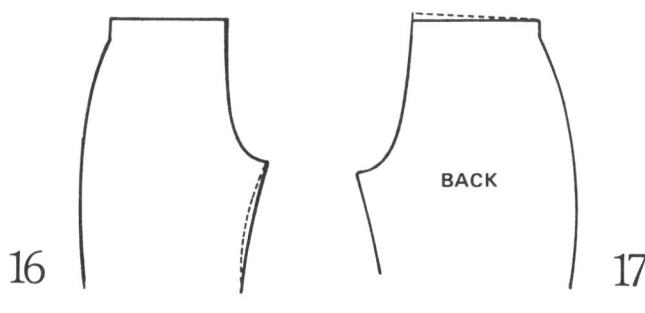

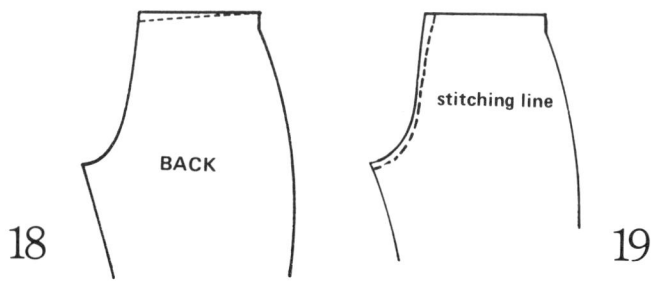

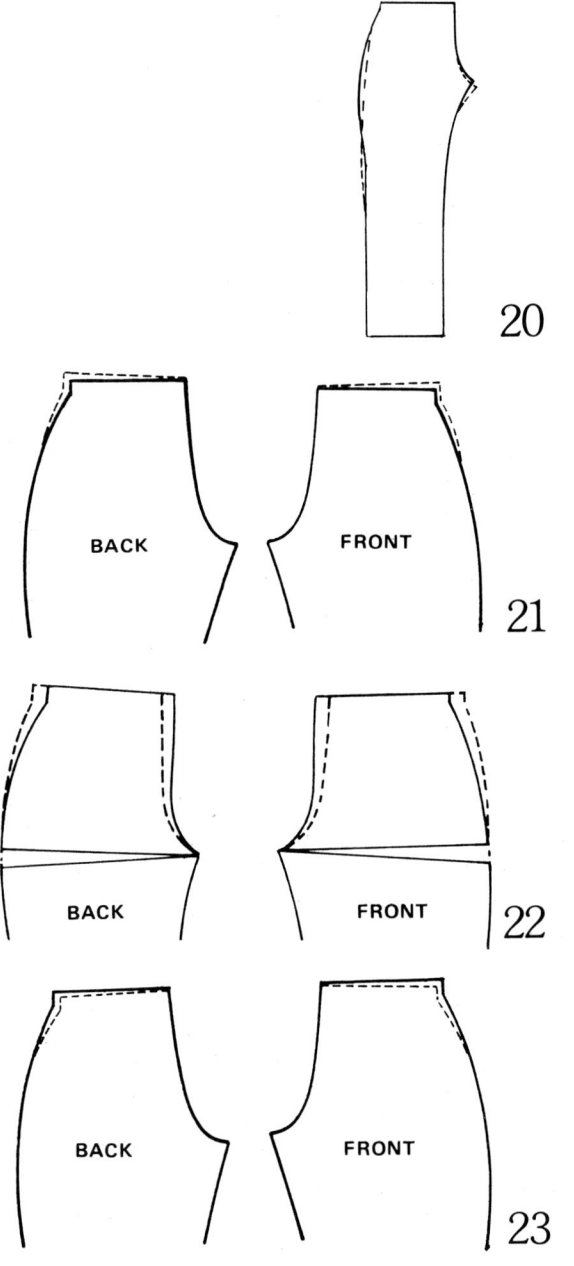

DROPPED SEAT

For a dropped seat, extra allowance will have to be made at the outside leg seam. A dropped seat is usually accompanied by a slim upper hip and for this you will need to redraw the pattern. Remove some of the upper curve of the hip on the front and back while adding, as previously mentioned, to the lower hip. Depending on the fullness of the figure, a slight extension of the back crotch shelf might also be necessary. (Fig. 20)

TWISTED LEGS FROM A HIGH HIP

If you have a high or especially full hip on one side, your pant crease will shift out rather than hang straight. More fabric is needed on that side to allow the pants to hang freely. It will be necessary to have a separate pattern for both the right and left side to correct this.

For a small adjustment (1/2 inch or less), lengthen the side seam and taper it toward the center front and center back seams on that side. Redraw the hip curve as illustrated. (Fig. 21)

For a larger adjustment, slash the pattern at the top of the inside leg seam and spread it the necessary amount. Redraw the hip curve according to the original pattern shape. (Fig. 22) This should be done on the front and back for that one side.

TWISTED LEGS FROM A LOW HIP

The reverse will occur when one hip is low or proportionately small. The pant crease will then swing in. Shorten the side seam and redraw the hip curve for a small adjustment. (Fig. 23) If more than 1/2 inch must be removed, a slash should be made at the top of the inside leg seam and lapped to swing the leg straight as illustrated.

DROPPED SEAT

TWISTED LEGS
FROM A HIGH HIP

TWISTED LEGS
FROM A LOW HIP

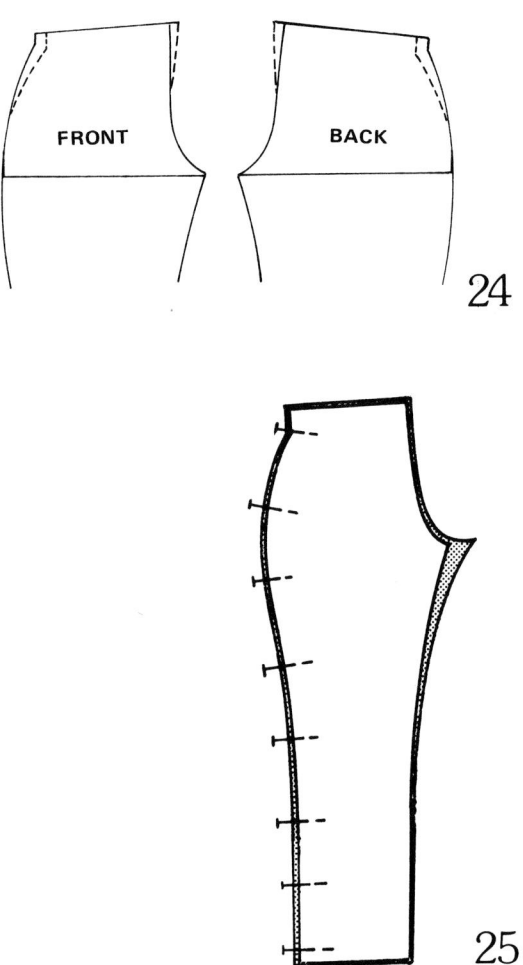

FRONT   BACK

24

25

Redraw the hip curve according to the original pattern shape. (Fig. 24)

TWISTED LEGS FROM UNEVEN STRETCHING

Generally, a twisted leg crease or seam is unrelated to a figure irregularity. The primary cause is stretching one layer of fabric more than the other. This happens if you do not take care in tracing the original pattern or in making adjustments to the crotch depth or leg length.

To avoid this common error, place your pattern pieces one on top of the other after they have been traced and cut from your pattern material. Pin the top of the pants together at the outside leg seam. Now, check your leg seams and see if they are exactly the same length. If these lines match, the seams will stitch together perfectly. If they do not match, trim the pattern material away from the longer one or add to the shorter one.

The stitching is always done from the bottom of the leg to the top. Pinning is important to prevent the tendency of the fabric to move. Place a pin every 8 inches while the pants are in a relaxed position on the cutting table. (Fig. 25)

These alterations are the ones most often used in making a better-fitting pair of women's pants. Always be careful to make small adjustments first. Too much fabric taken out here or added there can cause greater problems. The time spent on making a pattern for your figure that fits properly will be well worth the effort.

4

Pressing Your Pants

Pressing Your Pants

If there was only one word I could say that would tell you how to accomplish elegant garments when you are sewing in your home, it would be <u>press</u>. This very simple process that is such an important part of beautifully tailored clothes is often overlooked. So many times I have heard women say, "Oh, I haven't had time to really press this garment. I will get to it later." If you have waited until the garment is completed to do your pressing, you have waited too long. There is never a time when pressing is so important as in the initial stages of sewing. Each seam, as it is sewn, must be pressed.

Every time you sew a seam, think that I am standing there telling you to get up now and press that seam. I have had sewing rooms where my ironing board was positioned at the left of my sewing table and I simply swirled around in my chair to press my garment. This is a beautiful arrangement and if you ever have a chance to try it, see if it doesn't save you many hours of time in developing your beautiful wardrobe.

Always use a damp cloth when pressing the right side of your fabric. Synthetics melt at a low temperature and, without a pressing cloth, even a moderate iron may cause a shiny or slick surface. This shininess cannot be removed. It is also very important not to let your pressing action stretch the fabric. Remember: An over-pressed garment is as unattractive as a poorly-pressed garment.

Pressing to distribute hip fullness and pressing the creases require special attention. Because these procedures are so important, I would like to deal with them here.

PRESSING HIP FULLNESS

First, let us consider pressing the excess fullness from the hip. This is done after the outside leg seam has been sewn and <u>before</u> any construction takes place. After the seam has been carefully pressed open, use the steam of your iron to shrink out the bubble that appears over the hip. (Fig. 1) Beware, this is a shrinking process and not a stretching one.

Although it may not be noticeable, the shrinking process distributes ease in your pants. This is one of the interesting features of finishing knits that many people do not understand. Be sure to allow the steam to do the work for you. Don't actually press the area or you will stretch the fabric, causing your leg seams to swing in. (Fig. 2)

PRESSING CREASES

Pressing creases down the center front and center back is important to the total look of the pants. They should be sharp and straight. Pressing the creases is possible before or during construction. However, creases are often permanent in synthetics and, for this reason, you should not attempt to pre-crease your pants until the proper fit has been established. Each crease should always, without exception, fall halfway between the inside and outside leg seams.

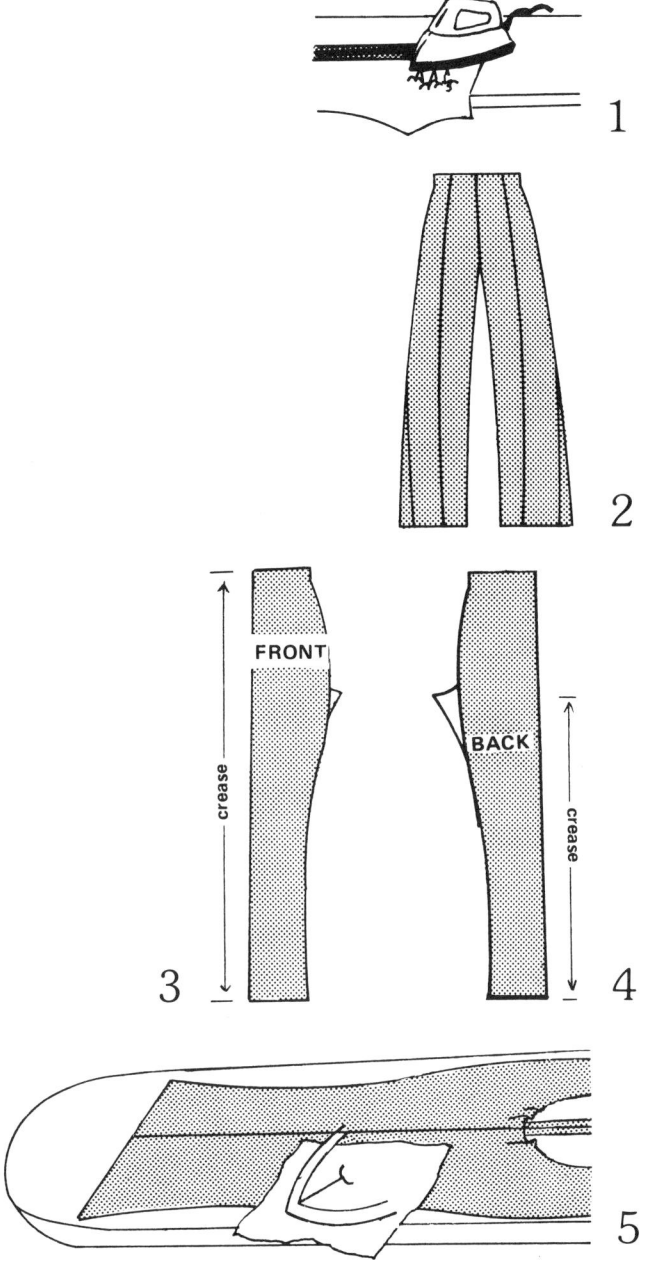

It is possible to press the creases in your pants before you do any sewing once you have made all the necessary fitting adjustments in your pattern. This is a simple way to create perfect creases. But, you must be certain that alterations will not be required later. Changing an outside leg seam could throw off the creases.

Take the separate front pieces and fold them exactly in half, matching inside and outside cut edges. (Fig. 3) The upper inside leg seam will extend slightly, as illustrated. Press each front section from the bottom to the top, using steam and a damp cloth. Allow the fabric to cool before continuing with construction. Many fibers relax when damp or hot so it is important to take a minute or two for them to cool and firm up.

Follow the same procedure to crease the two back sections. The crotch shelf will extend slightly farther in the back than in the front. (Fig. 4) The back crease should be pressed only to the top of the inside leg seam.

I prefer to press my creases at mid-construction, after I have sewn the outside and inside leg seams. At this point, the two pant legs have not yet been sewn together. Before pressing, try on one pant leg to check for any additional alterations. If they are needed, make these changes now.

Match the outside leg seams to the inside leg seams, keeping the straight of the fabric up the center front and center back. There will be a little extra fabric at the upper inside leg seam. This is the same fabric that extends when you press the creases before construction. (Fig. 5) Use a damp cloth and press. On the front, press from the bottom of the leg up to the waist. The crease should be on the center front line exactly halfway between the two leg seams. The crease up the back extends only to the top of the inside leg seam. Again, remember to let the fabric cool before continuing.

<u>You may press the creases in after construction</u>. One advantage to this is that you can try the pants on for a final fit, making any necessary alterations before pressing. Press the creases as you would during mid-construction, matching the outside leg seams to the inside leg seams. Set the crease in the front to the waist and in the back to the top of the inside leg seam. (Fig. 6)

PRESSING THE HEM

Pressing the hem carefully is often neglected in a pair of pants. If you sew your hem by hand, a good job of pressing will relieve a pulling down on the stitches and add strength to the hem. Otherwise, it will look as if you jumped into your pants as soon as you finished the last stitch.

I prefer to bond my hems. It is interesting to observe a group of men or women wearing knit pants. Hems done with *Perky Bond* fusible web always look crisp and well-pressed. This is not only because bonding requires careful pressing but, also, because *Perky Bond* adds body to the hem.

Pattern 700 allows for a 1-1/2 inch hem. If you are making your first pair of pants and are unsure about the finished length, try them on before completing the hem. Pin it in place and carefully press it. Then you may put in your hem by sewing it or bonding it with *Perky Bond*.

If you plan to bond your hem, tuck strips of *Perky Bond* inside the hem just below the raw edge after you have pressed the hem in place. Press, using a damp cloth and a hot iron. You must press until the cloth is dry in order to melt the nylon filament for a good, permanent bond.

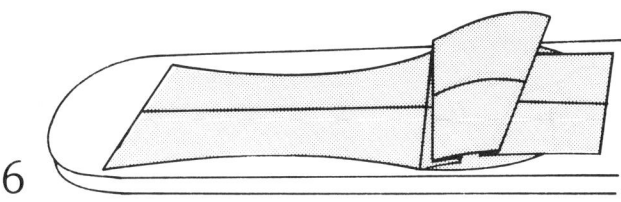

6

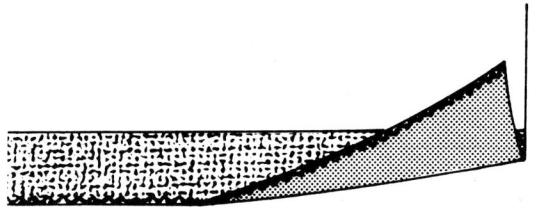

7

There is another easy way to bond a hem. First, press in the hem and then, machine-baste or zigzag *Perky Bond* to the inside edge. (Fig. 7) Press again as described above. This technique is excellent for all short hems like pant leg hems and sleeve hems.

The last step in constructing a beautifully finished garment is a complete pressing. Each crease should continue into a nice sharp edge at the hem. A careful job of final pressing will usually eliminate the need for additional pressing, even after many launderings.

5

Leg Variations and Cuffs

Leg Variations and Cuffs

Fashion changes in a pair of pants are quite often developed just by changing the shape of a leg. The western leg has for some time carried a flare, styled originally to accommodate the top of a riding boot. The typical mannish tailored look in pants calls for a fuller leg and perhaps, a pleat at the waistline. A crisp crease in a straight, untapered leg is always a flattering fashion pant. Tapering the pants at the knee, reminiscent of a rodeo trick rider costume, has had its influence as well.

Whatever the fashion may be, the important thing to keep in mind is how this will appear on your figure. One simple fact will influence your choice in pant styles. Vertical lines add height and horizontal lines shorten. Whenever you add curves, flares, pockets or do anything to break the lines of the straight leg, you will contribute to the illusion of shortening. If you wish to create a feeling of height and slimness, the straighter leg will be best for you.

The Stretch and Sew Slacks and Shorts Pattern 700 is designed with a perfectly straight leg which may be easily adapted to other styles. *Perky* Pattern Paper, a felt tip pen, yardstick, square, and fashion ruler are helpful in drafting new designs. When you are changing the leg style in slacks, certain rules should be kept in mind:

1. Any change that is made on the outside leg or the inside leg must be made identically on the back and front pattern pieces.

2. No matter what style change is made, the front and back outside leg seams and the front and back inside leg seams must be the same length.

3. Always stitch from the bottom to the top on any leg style.

4. Stretch every seam—equally—as you sew, no matter what the pant style.

WIDE STRAIGHT LEGS

While Pattern 700 features a straight leg, you might prefer to design a wide straight leg by adding fullness to the leg seams. To accomplish this, simply draw a line straight down from the widest point at the hip. Extend the same width to the inside leg seam at the bottom and draw a line straight up, parallel to the inside leg seam, to the crotch shelf. The crotch shelf should extend beyond this line for a smooth fit through the hips. Both lines should be parallel to the straight-of-grain line. (Fig. 1)

WIDE STRAIGHT LEGS
WITHOUT SIDE SEAMS

This look can be achieved by lapping and eliminating the outside leg seams of the pants. At the widest point of the hip, place the stitching lines of the seams directly on top of each other. The legs of the pant below this lap should be joined, and a dart should be made above the lap to maintain the fit without too much gathering. Keep the grain line on the front parallel to the grain line on the back. Measure the amount added

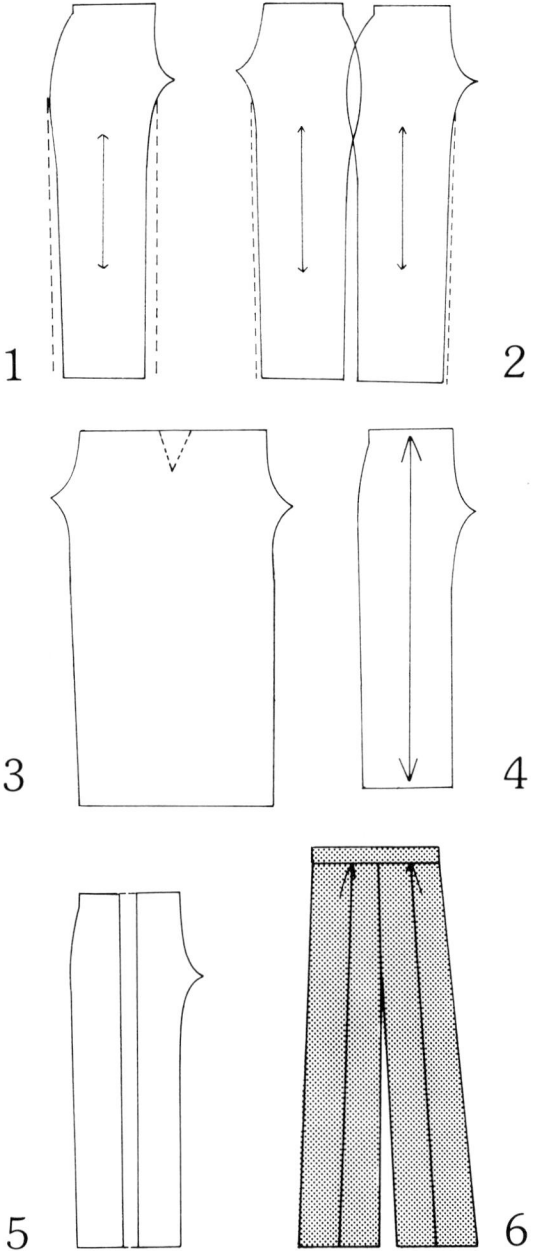

between the outside leg seams plus the two seam allowances and divide by two. Widen each leg at the inside leg seam this amount by drawing a line straight up to the crotch shelf. (Fig. 2) Redraw your pattern on *Do-Sew* pattern material or *Perky* Pattern Paper. (Fig. 3)

This is an especially effective way to cut pants from fabric that has an unevenness of design such as a diagonal or uneven plaid. The only matching necessary is at the center front and center back seams.

BAGGIES

For extra fullness in the front of pants, you may wish to add a pleat. Extend the straight-of-grain line on the <u>front</u> pattern piece to the waist and bottom edges. (Fig. 4) Cut on this line, separating the pattern front in half and place a 1-1/2 inch strip of *Perky* Pattern Paper behind the opening, taping it in place. (Fig. 5) Cut the front sections of your pants from this new pattern and construct them in the usual manner up to finishing the waist. Fold a 3/4 inch pleat at the top of the pants on the straight-of-grain line. The fold should go toward the side seams. If a crease is pressed in the front of the pants, it will fall directly into the line of the pleat. An applied waistband gives a finished look to this pant design. (Fig. 6)

LEGS FLARED AT THE SEAMLINES

Creating flare in a pant leg can be accomplished by simply tapering out the leg seams. Add the fullness you want equally on each side of both pattern pieces, beginning below the knee and tapering out to the bottom. (Fig. 7) Generally each seam is flared from 1 to 1-1/2 inches.

If you prefer a more exaggerated flare, taper your pattern to one size smaller at the knee. Bring the line back to your proper size and out to the desired flare. (Fig. 8) Remember: This should be done to both the front and back pattern pieces equally.

Flare may be added to the leg from the hip for a straighter and fuller effect. (Fig. 9) The degree of fullness is up to you. A palazzo or pajama leg is created if the leg is flared a great deal. Six to 8 inches of flare for each seam is an average amount for this look.

LEGS FLARED BY THE SLASH AND SPREAD TECHNIQUE

The slash and spread technique for creating flared legs is simpler than it appears and will give you more accuracy in leg shape than flaring from the seamlines. This handy method may be usefully applied to many style changes.

Draw your pattern on *Perky* Pattern Paper and cut three slashes on it from the bottom edge to the knee. (Fig. 10) Spread each slash equally, keeping the grain line arrow straight. Tiny folds will occur at the top of the slash points. You may have to compensate for this by adding extra length at the sides, but be sure to maintain a well-balanced curve at the hem. (Fig. 11) Redraw this altered pattern on *Perky* Pattern Paper or *Do-Sew* pattern material.

For a fuller leg, straighten the inside and outside leg seams from the hip (just below the crotch shelf) to the bottom edge. (Fig. 12) Slash your pattern in three places as illustrated (Fig. 12) and spread each slash equally to the desired fullness. (Fig. 13) When the pattern is spread, a curve will occur at the bottom edge of the leg, giving the pants good overall balance.

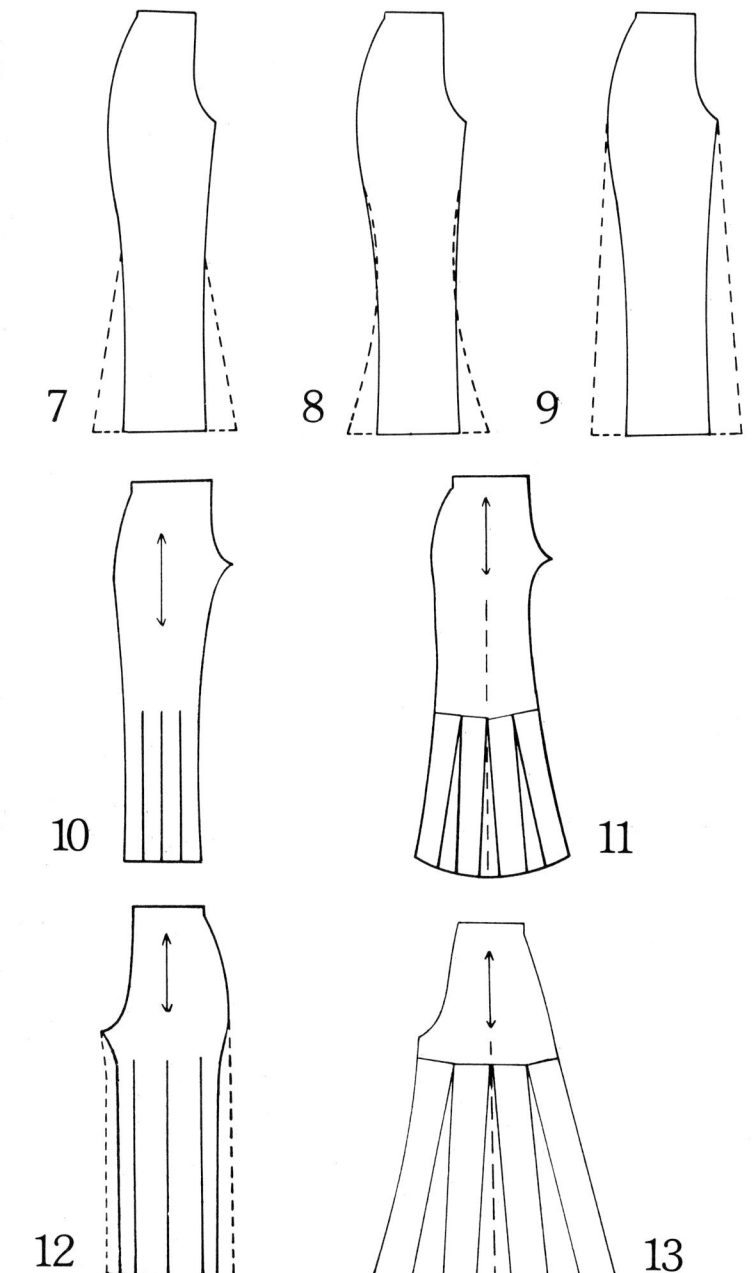

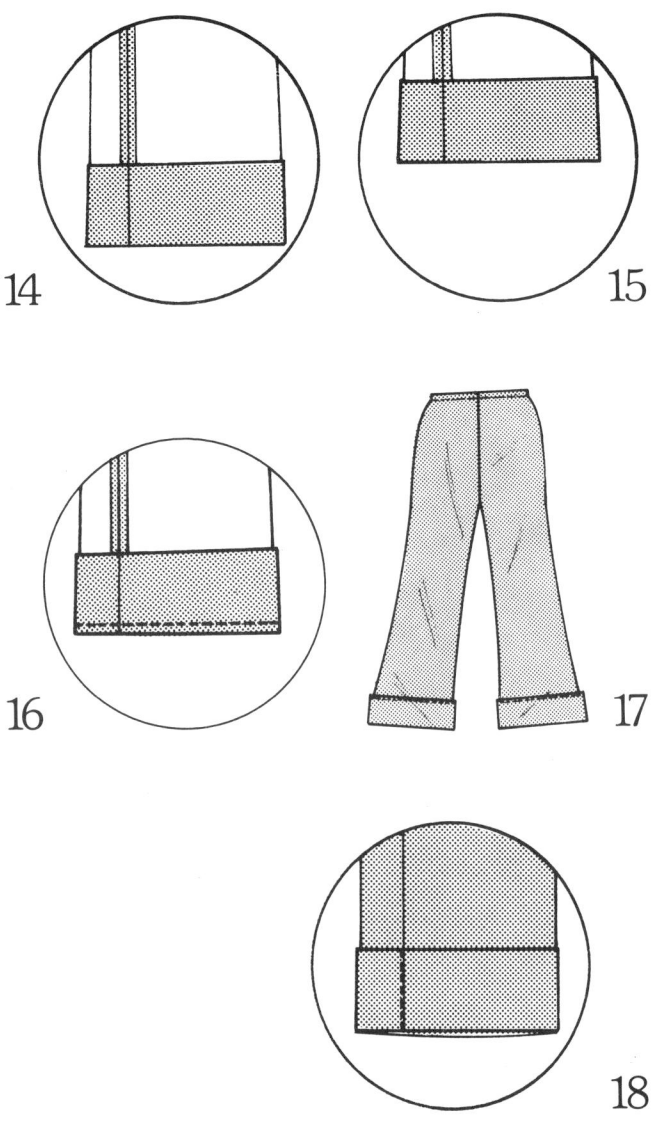

14

15

16

17

18

Redraw your pattern on *Perky* Pattern Paper or *Do-Sew* pattern material.

FAKE CUFFS ON PANT LEGS

For a 1-1/2 inch decorative but fake cuff, add 1/2 inch to the length of your pattern. A 1-1/2 inch hem has been allowed so, totally, you will need 2 inches more than your finished length. After constructing the garment, fold 1-1/2 inches at the bottom edge of the pant leg to the wrong side. (Fig. 14) Press carefully. Again, fold 1-1/2 inches to the wrong side and press. (Fig. 15) Notice that the cut edge at the bottom of the leg is resting in the second fold. Stitch 1/4 inch from the edge of the second fold line, taking care that the cut edge is caught inside this stitching. (Fig. 16) Fold the cuff down and press the 1/4 inch seam up toward the knee. The technique is completed and you have a lovely garment with the appearance of having a cuff. (Fig. 17) It's simple and such fun to do!

CUFFS

For a 2-inch wide cuff on the straight leg design of Stretch and Sew Pattern 700, additional fabric will be needed at the bottom. The pattern calls for a 1-1/2 inch hem at the bottom of the leg. If you have your pattern adjusted to the proper length for you with a 1-1/2 inch hem, you will need to lengthen your pattern 4 inches. This will provide a total of 5-1/2 inches of fabric in addition to your finished length.

After constructing the garment, fold the bottom hem up 3-1/2 inches to the wrong side of each leg. Press and stitch the hem or bond it in place with *Perky Bond.* Then fold the bottom 2 inches to the right side for the cuff. Press and stitch-in-the-ditch on each side seam. (To stitch-in-the-ditch is to stitch from the right side directly in the seamline.) This will hold your cuff beautifully in place. (Fig. 18)

CUFFS FOR LEGS
FLARED AT THE SEAMLINES

For a 2-inch wide cuff on a leg flared at the seamlines from the knee, a slightly different technique must be used than for cuffs on pants with straight or relatively straight legs. Mark the finished length on your pants pattern. Fold a 22x22 inch piece of dotted *Perky* Pattern Paper 3 inches on one edge (Fig. 19) and then fold it again in the opposite direction 2 inches. (Fig. 20) Place the bottom fold of the dotted paper on the finished length line of your pants pattern and pin or tape it in place. To create the flare, measure out 1 to 1-1/2 inches from the inside and outside leg seams at the bottom. Draw a line up to the knee or just below the knee. (Fig. 21) Following this line, cut the *Perky* Pattern Paper and you will have your pattern. (Fig. 22) You must make a pattern of this type for both the front and back.

Sew the pants in the usual manner but follow the new lines of the pattern leg. Fold the fabric 3 inches to the wrong side and hem. Then, fold 2 inches to the right side just as you did the paper pattern and you will have a cuff that contours beautifully to the flare design. Press and stitch-in-the-ditch on each side seam.

CUFFS FOR LEGS FLARED
BY SLASHING AND SPREADING

For a 2-inch wide cuff on a leg flared by slashing, you must add 4 inches to the bottom of the flare. Do not continue the flare in this extension but draw straight down from the leg. (Fig. 23) Follow the previous instructions for folding a cuff and then carefully press it, shaping it and steaming out any extra fullness at the top.

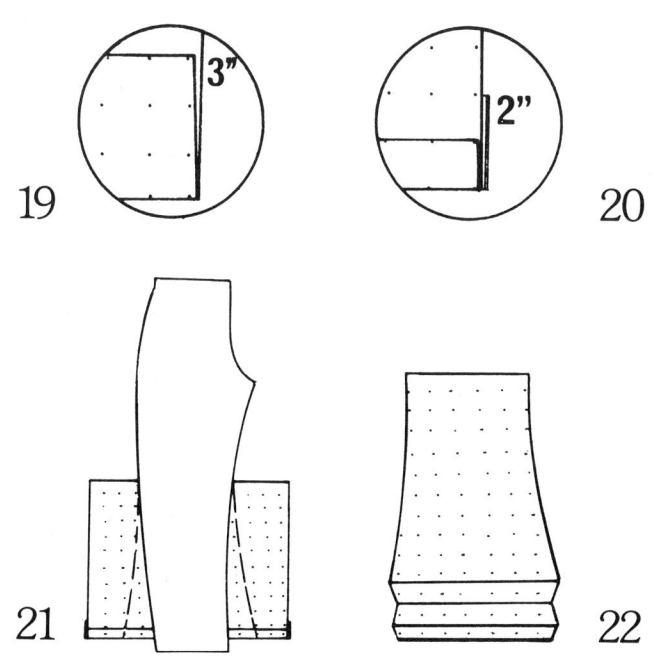

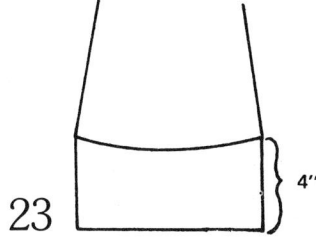

Creativity, in my opinion, is something old made new, and originality is the ability to get an idea and put it to work for you. Ideas could be inspired by many things you see in your day-to-day activities. For instance, I enjoy studying fashion magazines—European as well as American. With a little courage, you'll be on your way to a wardrobe of beautifully designed pants you have truly done yourself.

6

Yokes and Pockets

Yokes and Pockets

We want to give you some ideas about how to add a pocket detail to your regular pants pattern and how to vary the pocket in the Jeans Pattern. You should allow a little extra ease in pants with yokes or pockets. This is important as they tend to stabilize the pants and, if the pants are tight over the hip area, they will not be attractive. So, for the final detail of a custom garment, you will enjoy learning many of the little tricks to changing a garment and creating something that is your very own.

YOKES

If you wish to do some creative designing of your own by adding a yoke to the pants, the simplest and safest way is to first trace your pants pattern on *Perky* Pattern Paper. Mark in all seam allowances. (Fig. 1) This will help you achieve a truer picture of your style design. Draw on the pattern the yoke style you wish to add. (Fig. 2)

With a fresh piece of dotted *Perky* Pattern Paper or *Do-Sew* pattern material (for a permanent pattern), trace each individual piece. Add a seam allowance to each seam that is not already marked for seam allowance. If the yoke is at all complicated, position some notches on the pattern pieces to ensure that you properly assemble them. (Fig. 3) If you draw a yoke with a pointed design, it will be necessary to clip at each point and pivot as you sew.

Topstitching the yoke after it has been sewn to the pants can be quite attractive. Try using thread of contrasting color for an added dimen-

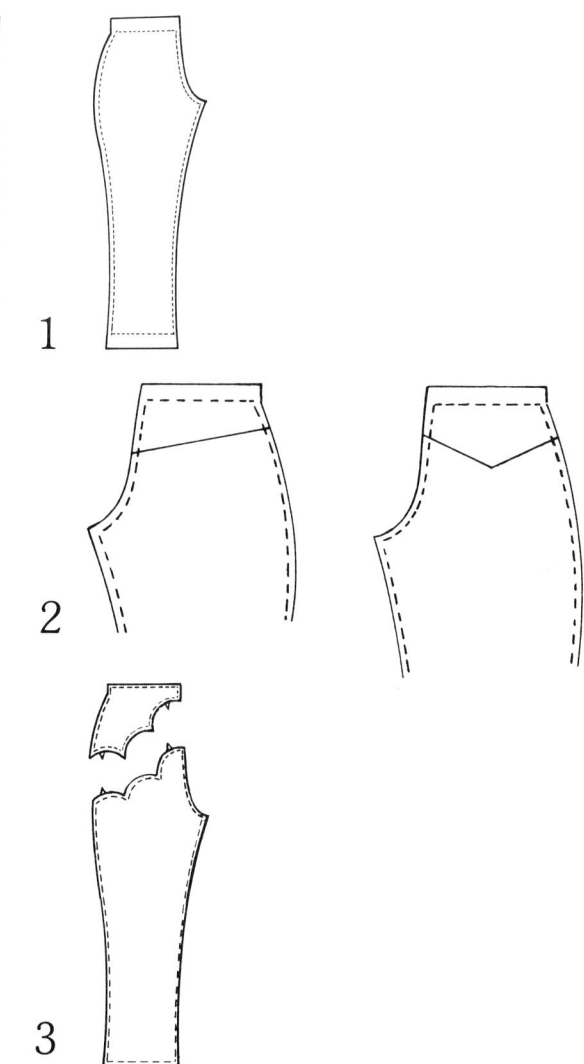

1

2

3

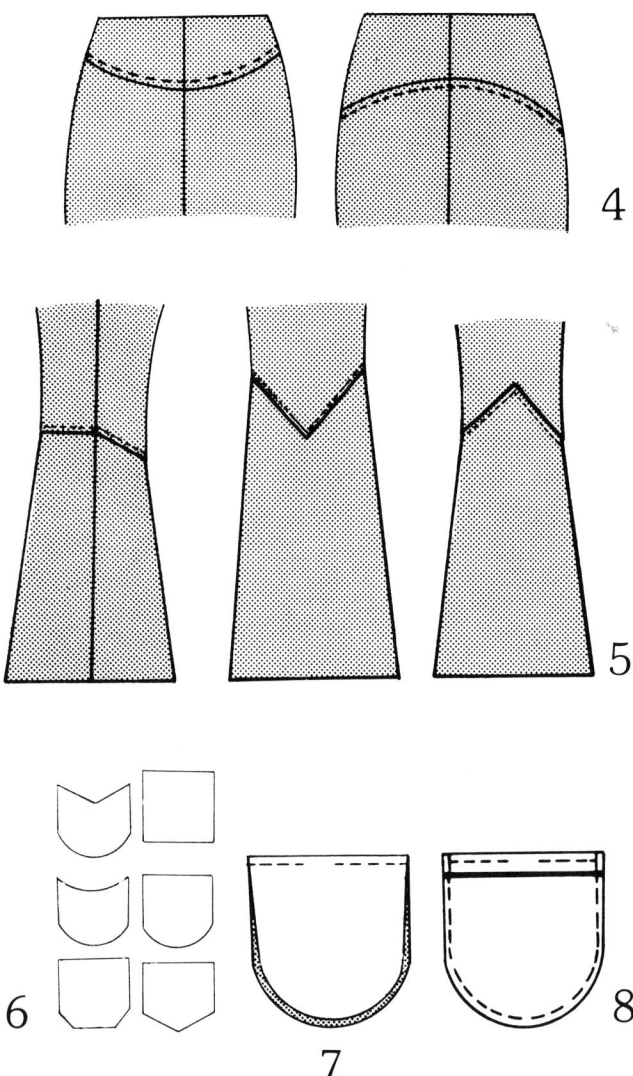

sion. In determining the direction to press the seam before topstitching, I usually follow the way of least resistance. (Fig. 4)

Follow the same procedure for a design at the knee as you did for a yoke. Remember to add seam allowance to each design cut edge before sewing your pants together. This is an attractive variation on a straight or flared leg. Topstitching as well as the use of contrasting fabrics adds an interesting touch. (Fig. 5)

PATCH POCKET

Patch pockets sewn on the front or back are a nice addition to pants. Start with a square of fabric that measures approximately 6-1/4 inches by 6-1/4 inches. Shape the bottom or top any way you like. (Fig. 6) Cut a lining from *Perky Bond Plus* fusible interfacing fabric, or a lightweight fabric. Use the same pattern for the pocket lining, but subtract 5/8 inch from the top and 1/8 inch from the sides and bottom.

Place the lining on the pocket, right sides together. (The non-adhesive side is the right side of *Perky Bond Plus*.) Stitch across the top, easing the extra pocket fabric into the lining. Leave 1-1/2 inches open in the center for turning. (Fig. 7) Pull the lining down to match the edges of the pocket. This will provide a fold rather than the sewn seam to finish the top of the pocket. The seam will be 5/8 inch to the inside. Stitch the two pieces together. (Fig. 8)

Clip the corners and turn the pocket to the right side through the opening in the top of the pocket. The pocket will extend slightly over the edges of the lining due to the smaller size of the lining. Press the pocket carefully. If *Perky Bond Plus* has been used, this pressing will fuse the two pieces together. Remember, to make a permanent bond, use a damp cloth with your hot iron.

Your pocket is ready to sew to your garment. First, you might like to sew a line of topstitching around the entire pocket 1/4 inch from the edge. Stitch the pocket to the pants 1/8 inch from the pocket edge, reinforcing the top corners. (Fig. 9)

FLAP POCKET

If you prefer a patch pocket with a flap, extend the length of the pocket described above by 2 inches. Cut both pocket pieces the identical size and sew them, right sides together. Leave 1-1/2 inches along one side for turning. (Fig. 10) Clip the corners and turn the pocket to the right side through the opening. Press it carefully and topstitch the <u>flap</u> 1/4 inch from the edge. (Fig. 11) Position the pocket on the garment and stitch, reinforcing each top corner. This stitching should also be 1/4 inch from the edge to match the flap. Turn the flap down and finish with a decorative button. (Fig. 12)

CONTINENTAL POCKET

The continental pocket is a favorite for women's pants. You may use the pocket pattern from the Tennis Shorts Pattern 650. Or, to draw your own, use the front from your pants pattern as a guide.

Trace the upper portion of your front onto a piece of *Perky* Pattern Paper or *Do-Sew*. Starting at the top of the side seam, measure the pocket width across the top of the pattern (approximately 6 inches). Draw a line straight down to the desired pocket depth (approximately 10 to 11 inches) and curve this line to meet the side seam. (Fig. 13) This will be your under pocket pattern piece.

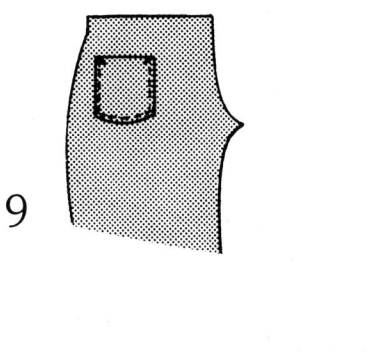

9

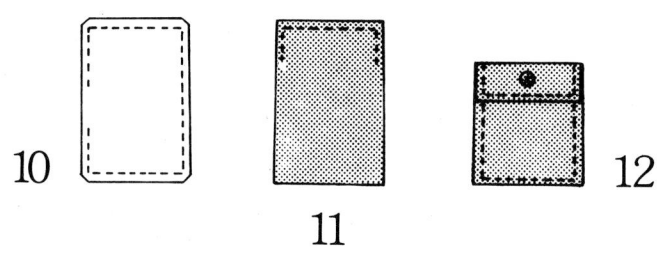

10   11   12

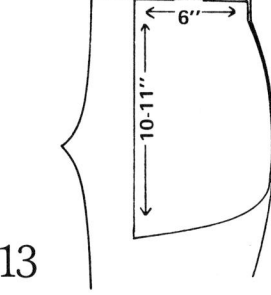

13

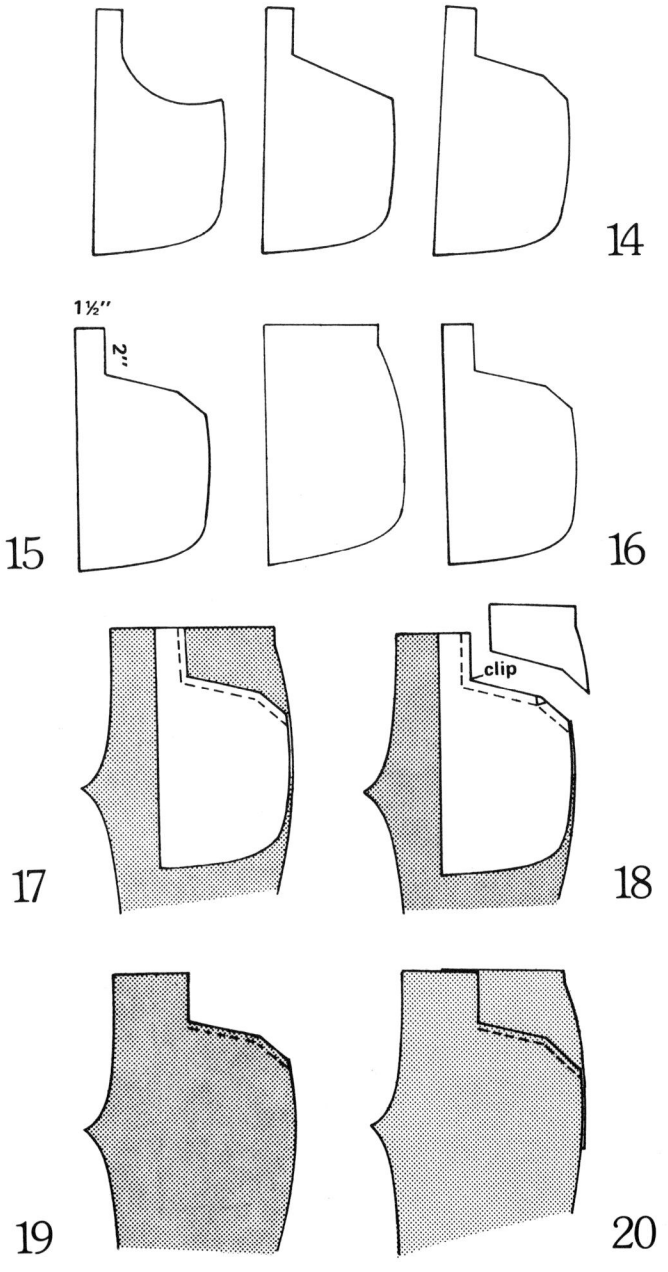

Make an additional under pocket pattern piece. You will design your upper pocket from this. The upper pocket determines the shape of the finished pocket opening. It can be curved, straight, or angular. (Fig. 14)

In drawing your upper pocket, first measure on your under pocket piece 1-1/2 inches from the inside edge and draw a line 2 inches straight down from that point. This will allow the pocket to extend enough at the top for the turned-down elastic waist finish. (Fig. 15) However, if you are using the pocket in conjunction with an applied waistband, subtract 7/8 inch from the vertical measurement. The line you draw from this point to your seamline will determine your pocket style.

You now have two pocket pattern pieces. (Fig. 16) Cut one upper and one under pocket piece for each pocket.

To apply the pockets to the pants, position the upper pocket on the pants front, right sides together, matching them at the side seam and the top. Stitch the top edge of the upper pocket with a 5/8 inch seam allowance (Fig. 17) and trim the pants fabric even with it. Clip the seam allowance at the inside corner and, when you are using the angular design illustrated, cut a wedge from the seam allowance at the outside corner. (Fig. 18) If you have chosen a curved pocket, trim the entire seam. Press the seam allowance open and then turn the upper pocket to the inside and press. Topstitch 1/4 inch from the pocket edge, with the stitching line extending from the side seam to the inside corner. (Fig. 19)

Place the under pocket behind the finished upper pocket. The under pocket will fill in the pants top that was trimmed away. It should be even with the upper pocket on all cut edges. (Fig. 20)

Fold back the pants at the center front, exposing the seam allowances of the pocket. Sew on the previous stitching line to secure the under pocket to the upper pocket. (Fig. 21) On the right side, complete the topstitching so that it will meet the previous topstitching line. (Fig. 22) Complete the pocket by sewing around the raw edges. Zigzag a second row of stitching for extra stability. (Fig. 23)

WELT POCKET

A welt pocket is most often used in the back of women's pants, but it can also be adapted to be placed in front. A pocket lining will add stability to the finished pocket and will serve as a stay while you sew the welt.

From the pocket lining fabric, cut a pocket stay the size of the finished pocket plus 1 inch seam allowances on the sides and bottom and with a 3 to 4 inch extension on the top. Three inches is fine if you apply a separate waistband. Four inches is needed with the turned-down elastic finish. On the pocket stay, draw a box the finished size of the pocket opening (approximately 1/2 inch by 5 inches) with at least 3 to 4 inches of the stay above the box and 1 inch on each side. Draw a cutting line along the center of the box and draw wedges at least 1/2 inch long at each end of the box. (Fig. 24)

If you are putting the welt pocket in the back, position the stay on the right side of the pants back so that the pocket opening is 2 inches in from the side seam and 3 to 4 inches down from the top cut edge. Pin it in place. Stitch around the box, sewing on the stay fabric, using 12 stitches to the inch. Pivot carefully at each corner. Be sure the stitches overlap where you begin and end sewing so there is no chance they will pull out. (Fig. 25)

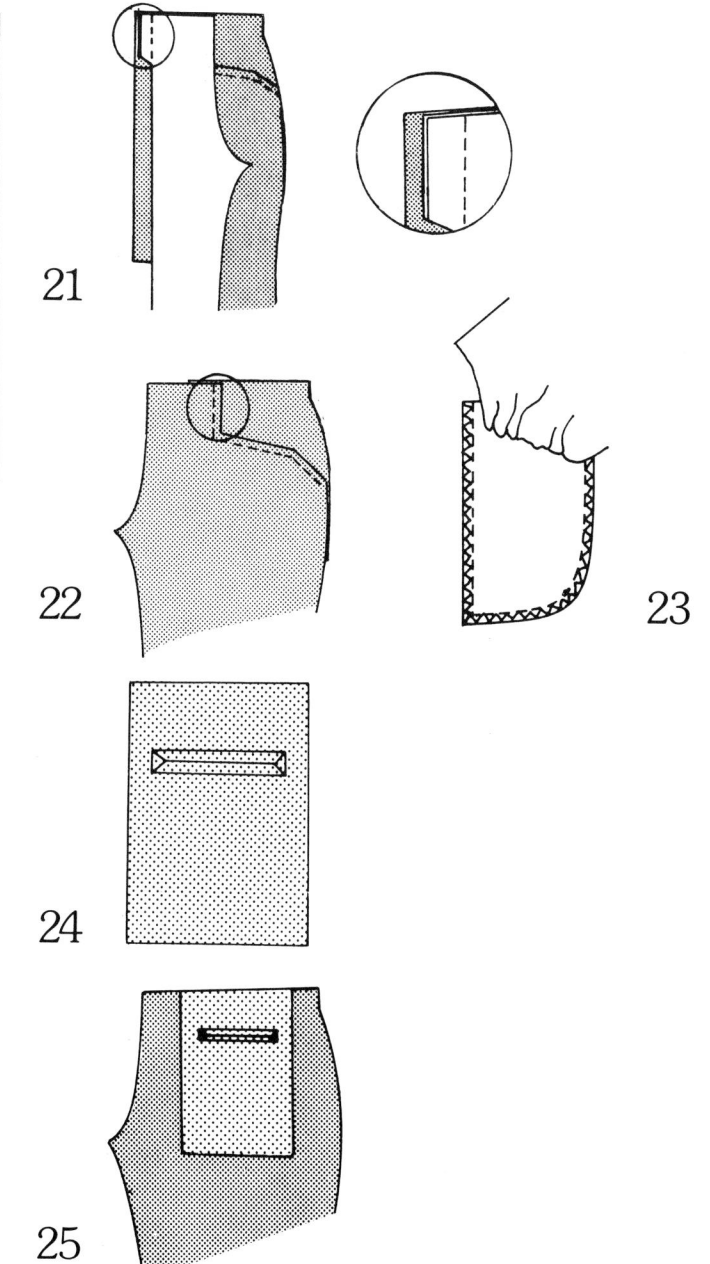

21

22

23

24

25

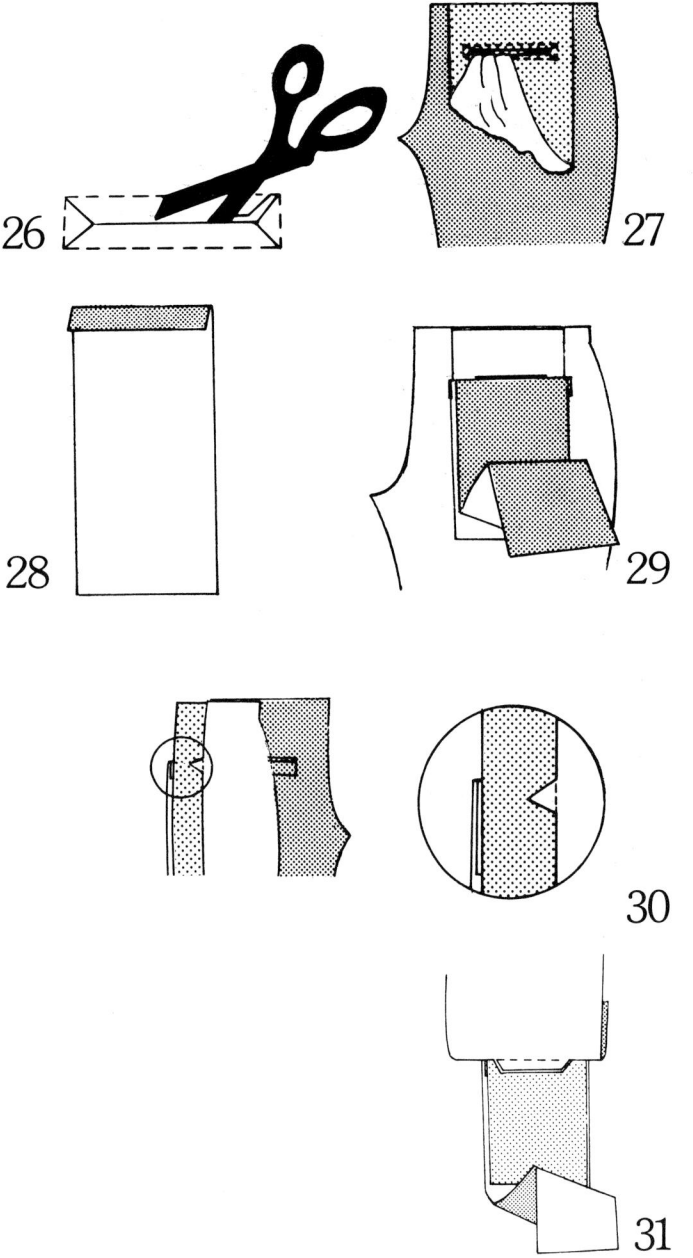

Cut down the center of the box on the stay's cutting line, through the garment and the stay. Clip sharply into the corners, forming a wedge at each end of the box, but take care not to cut the stitches. (Fig. 26)

Turn the stay to the inside of the garment through the box. (Fig. 27) Press the stay with your steam iron, making sure none of the stay fabric shows from the right side of the garment.

The pocket is made in one continuous strip as wide as the pocket opening plus 2 inches and twice the depth of the finished pocket plus 4 to 5 inches. If you like, you may apply *Perky Bond Plus* to the wrong side of the pocket for extra reinforcement.

To form the pocket welt, fold one end of the pocket down 1 inch, wrong sides together. A strip of *Perky Bond* positioned under the folded end and bonded will enable you to work with the pocket welt more easily. (Fig. 28)

Place the welt behind the pocket opening with the welt completely filling the box and the folded edge of the welt even with the top of the box. It's helpful to position the welt with transparent tape instead of pins to keep the welt from slipping out of position. (Fig. 29)

Fold back the garment fabric to expose the wedge at the end of the box. Stitch across the end, sewing through the wedge, the pocket stay, and the welt from the bottom up to the fold. Sew the other end in the same way. (Fig. 30)

Fold up the bottom of the garment, exposing the seam at the lower edge of the box. Stitch this seam, sewing through the seam allowance, the pocket stay, and the welt. (Fig. 31)

Position the cut end of the pocket so that it extends up beyond the pocket welt and is even with the cut edge at the waist. Press the pocket carefully into position. (Fig. 32) Fold the garment down and stitch the upper seam of the box in the same manner as you did the lower seam, catching both layers of the pocket. (Fig. 33)

Using a straight stitch, sew all the way around the pocket, rounding the lower corners to prevent lint from collecting. A second stitching is necessary for reinforcement. I like to use a multiple zigzag stitch for this. However, a zigzag stitch or a second row of straight stitching would work perfectly well. (Fig. 34) Baste the upper pocket edge to the waist edge. Press the pocket carefully.

Finally, a row of topstitching through all thicknesses, 1/4 inch above the box will help keep the pocket in place and give it a sharp appearance. (Fig. 35)

WELT POCKET FOR LIGHTWEIGHT PANTS

If you are using a lightweight fabric and need strength for your pocket but less bulk, you might like to try this welt pocket. *Perky Bond Plus* will serve as a stay while you sew this welt and it will add stability to the finished pocket.

From the *Perky Bond Plus*, cut a pocket stay the size of the finished pocket plus 1-inch seam allowances on the sides and bottom and with a 3 to 4-inch extension on the top. Three inches is fine if you apply a separate waistband. Four inches is needed with the turned-down elastic finish. On the non-adhesive side, draw a box 4 to 6 inches long and 1/4 inch wide with at least 3 to 4 inches of the stay above the box and 1 inch on each side. Draw a cutting line along the center of the box and draw wedges at least 1/4 inch long at each end of the box. (Fig. 36)

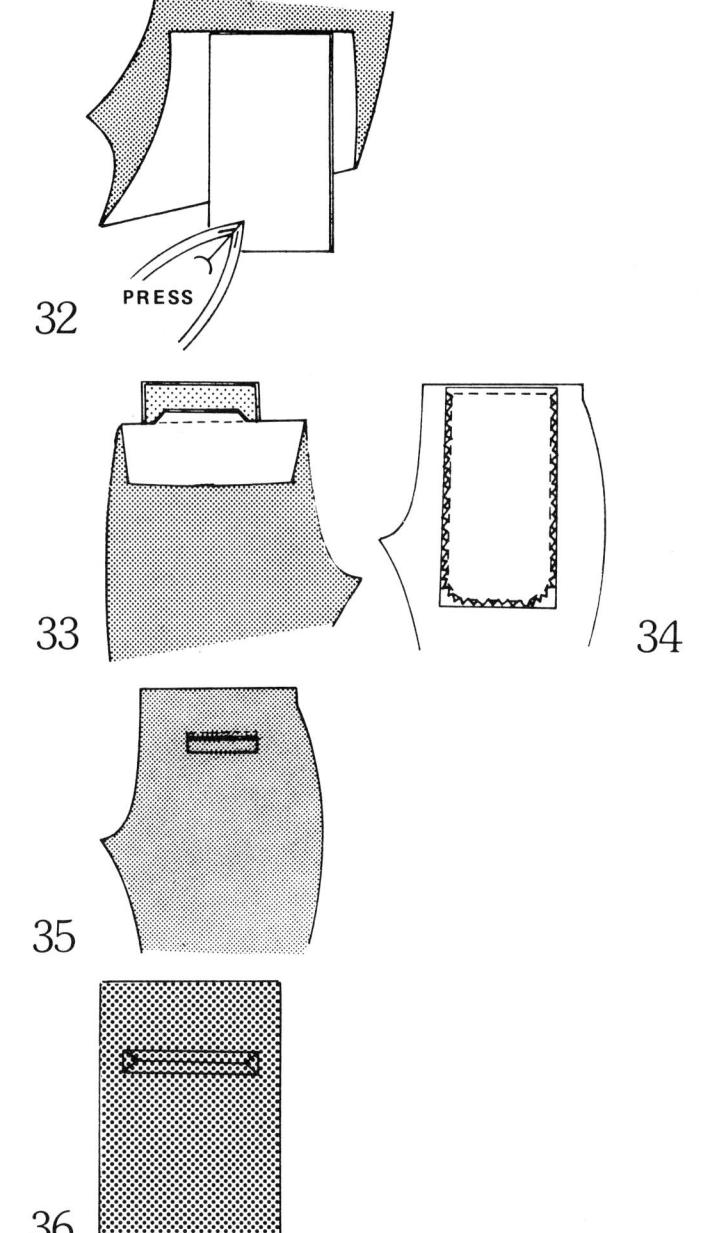

32 PRESS

33

34

35

36

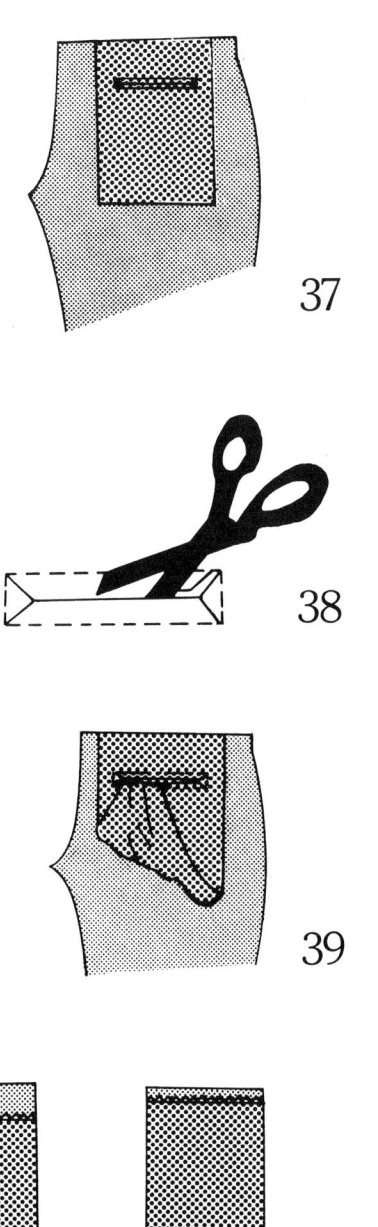

37

38

39

40   41

If you are putting the welt pocket in the back, position the stay on the right side of the pants back so that the pocket opening is 2 inches in from the side seam and 3 to 4 inches down from the top cut edge. The adhesive side of the stay should be next to the right side of the pants. Pin it in place. Stitch around the box, sewing on the stay fabric, using 12 stitches to the inch. Pivot carefully at each corner. Be sure the stitches overlap where you begin and end sewing so there is no chance that they will pull out. (Fig. 37)

Cut down the center of the box on the stay's cutting line through the garment and the stay. Clip sharply into the corners, forming a wedge at each end of the box, but take care not to cut the stitches. (Fig. 38)

Turn the stay to the inside of the garment through the box. (Fig. 39) Finger-press the stay from the right side so that it does not show. Do not press with an iron.

From pocket lining, cut a strip that is as wide as the pocket opening plus 2 inches and twice the depth of the finished pocket plus 4 inches. From your pants fabric, cut 2 rectangles, each measuring the width of the pocket opening plus 2 inches. One should be 2 inches in length. It will serve as the pocket welt. The welt facing should be 3 inches in length.

Apply *Perky Bond Plus* to the wrong side of the pocket welt. Lap one edge of the bonded strip 1/4 inch over the right side of the lining fabric and stitch with a zigzag stitch. (Fig. 40) Fold the welt in half lengthwise, with wrong sides together. Lap 1/4 inch over the wrong side of the lining and zigzag again over the previous stitching line. (Fig. 41) Press carefully.

Place the wrong side of the welt facing on the right side of the lining, 3 inches from the edge. Pin and stitch it in place. (Fig. 42) Position the welt behind the box with the wrong side of the lining against the wrong side of the pants. Fill the opening with the folded edge of the welt. (Fig. 43)

Fold the pants back at each end, exposing the wedges. Apply the *Perky Bond Plus* to the lining by pressing each wedge, using a damp pressing cloth and a hot iron. Then, fold the pants up from the bottom, exposing the seam allowance at the lower edge of the box and carefully press to bond. (Fig. 44)

To stitch the welt in place, fold the pants back at each end, exposing the wedge. Sew across each wedge. (Fig. 45) Then sew across the stitching line at the bottom of the original box. (Fig. 46)

Fold the pocket from the lower edge up to the waist edge. The welt facing should be at the pocket opening. Press in place. (Fig. 47) Fold the garment down and stitch the upper seam of the box in the same manner as you did the lower seam, catching both layers of the pocket. (Fig. 48)

Using a straight stitch, sew all the way around the pocket, rounding the lower corners to prevent lint from collecting. A second stitching is necessary for reinforcement. I like to use a multiple zigzag stitch for this. However, a zigzag stitch or a second row of straight stitching would work perfectly well. (Fig. 49) Baste the upper pocket edge to the waist edge. Press the pocket carefully.

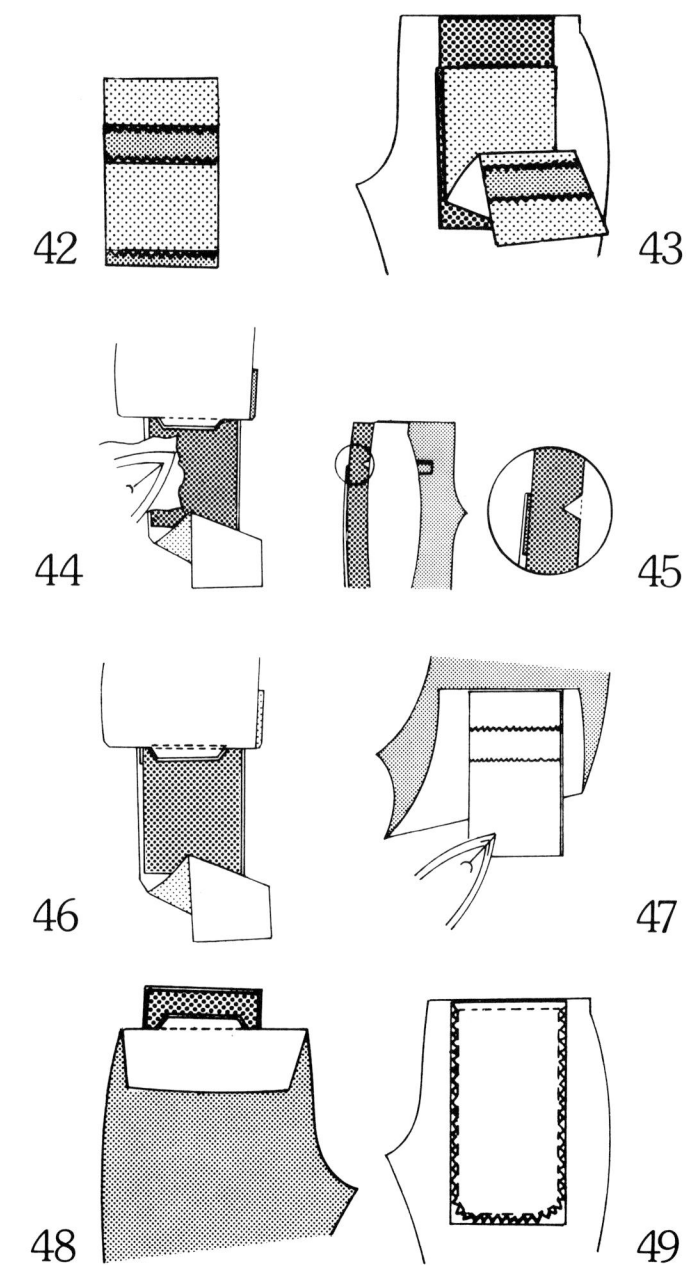

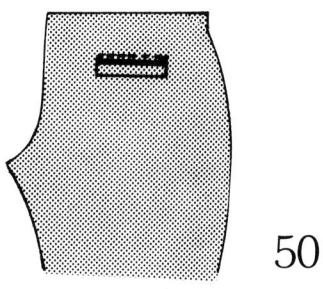

50

Finally, a row of topstitching, through all thicknesses 1/4 inch above the box, will help keep the pocket in place and give it a sharp appearance. (Fig. 50)

A yoke here, a pocket there, simple little variations that can lend so much to a fashion look in pants. Again, you will see the western influence in many of the details as well as in the patch pockets. Once you have worn pants with roomy pockets, you will find you are spoiled for pants that do not have pockets.

Flies and Waistbands

Flies and Waistbands

Fashion seems to be in a constant turmoil of change. As soon as we become accustomed to a certain style change, we find a new look has emerged and we are suddenly amazed to realize that our tastes have swung with the new trend and we are ready for the new look.

As we see fashion changing, we feel a need for variations. The waistband of the pull-on pants is perfect with the turned-under elastic. Yet, if you wish to wear a body blouse or tuck-in blouse, you will want a more finished appearance at the waist. Often a casing with the elastic enclosed is sufficient. But if the fabric is fairly stable, a placket might be needed as well. Just for the detail, you may find the need of the fly front enclosure. These are all techniques that we will deal with here.

FAKE FLY

You might like to add a fake fly to your slacks. The fly may be used in conjunction with the waistband without a closure described in a following section or with the waist finish described in the pattern instructions. A facing must be added to the front pattern piece. Measure 1-1/2 inches out from the center front seamline and connect this point to a curved line drawn out from the seamline approximately 3 inches up from the inside leg seam. (Fig. 1) This will be your fly facing. Cut both front sections from this adjusted pattern.

Place the two front sections right sides together. Stitch on the seamline from a point 1-1/2

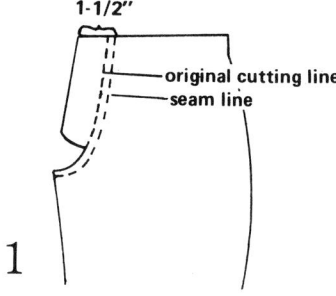

1-1/2"

original cutting line
seam line

1

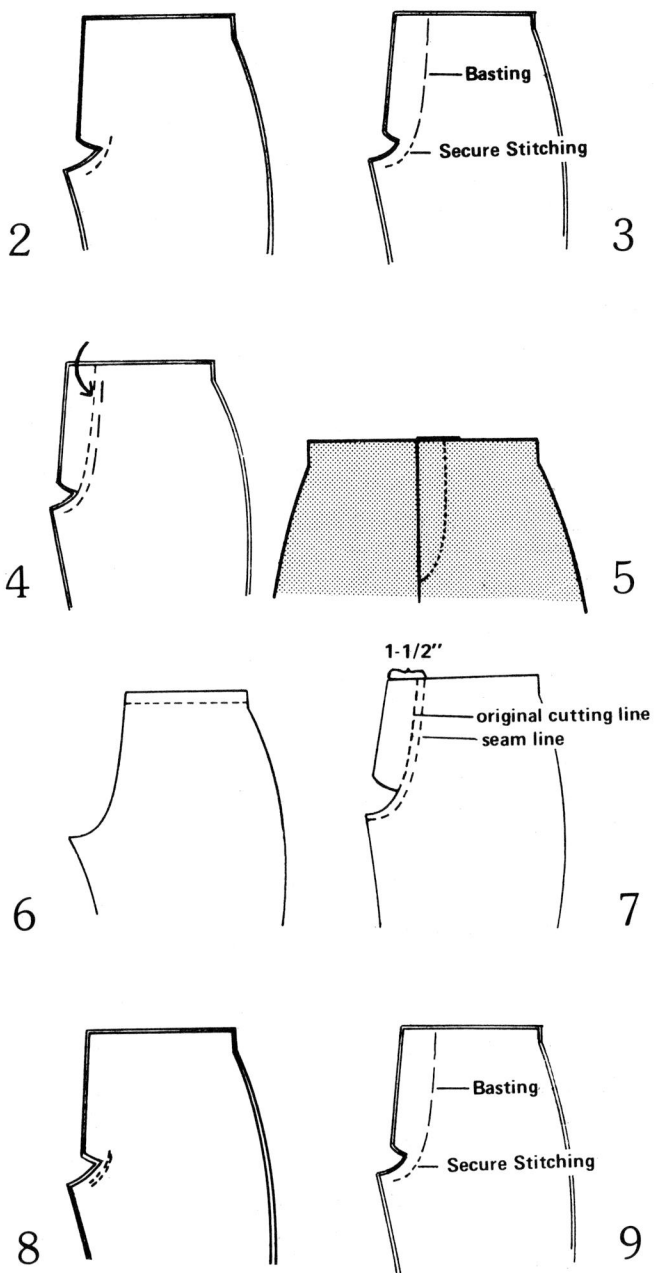

2 — Basting — Secure Stitching 3

4 — 5

1-1/2"

6 — original cutting line — seam line 7

8 — Basting — Secure Stitching 9

inches from the inside leg seam to a point approximately 5/8 inch above the start of the fly facing. (Fig. 2) With a machine basting stitch, continue sewing on the seamline to the top of the pants. (Fig. 3) Sew with your regular stitch length a line of stitching 5/8 inch from the basting line on the original cut edge. (Fig. 4) Open the pants front, folding the double facing to the left, and stitch the fly from the right side. (Fig. 5) Remove the basting stitches and you will have an attractive fake fly. Buttons may be added for fashion variety.

FLY WITH ZIPPER

Since a waistband is usually added to pants with a zipper opening, subtract 7/8 inch from the waistline edge of the front and back pattern pieces. (Fig. 6) This will leave a 5/8 inch seam allowance for the addition of a waistband and closure. Add a fly facing to your pants pattern in the same way as you do for the fake fly in the preceding section. (Fig. 7)

To sew the fly, place the two front sections, right sides together. Stitch on the original seamline from a point 1 inch from the inside leg seam to a point approximately 5/8 inch above the start of the fly facing. A second row of stitching right next to the first will strengthen this stress seam. (Fig. 8) With a machine basting stitch, continue sewing to the top of the pants. (Fig. 9) Clip into the seam at the bottom of the fly section. (Fig. 10)

Fold the fronts and the <u>left</u> fly section to one side. Position the zipper face down on the right fly facing section so that the edge of the zipper tape is resting against the basted center seam. The zipper tape that extends below the zipper teeth should be even with the bottom edge of the fly facing. Using the zipper foot on your machine, sew along the right side of the zipper next to the zipper teeth. Stitch only through the zipper tape and the right fly facing section. (Fig. 11)

With the pants lying flat, lift the unstitched zipper tape that is resting against the basted center seam and shift the zipper to the left fly facing. The zipper will be in the same position on the left fly facing as it was on the right fly facing. Sew along the left side of the zipper tape next to the zipper teeth. Stitch only through the zipper tape and left fly facing. (Fig. 12)

Position the entire fly facing section flat against the left front. From the right side, topstitch through all thicknesses. Start by forming a curve at the bottom of the zipper. The remainder of the stitching should be 1-1/4 inches from the center front. (Fig. 13) Remove the basting stitches from the center front seam and press the fly carefully.

Cut a zipper guard from a strip of self-fabric that measures 3 inches by 9 inches. Fold the zipper guard lengthwise with the wrong sides together and press. A strip of *Perky Bond* inserted into the fold before you press will offer more stability to the zipper guard and make application easier.

Place the zipper guard behind the open zipper on the right fly facing section with the raw edges of the zipper guard even with the raw edge of the facing. Topstitch 1/8 inch from the zipper teeth. (Fig. 14) Close the zipper and lift the pants, exposing the end of the zipper and the fabric guard. Sew across the bottom through all these thicknesses. Trim any extending fabric to 1/2 inch. (Fig. 15) You will trim the excess zipper at the top after you have sewn on your waistband.

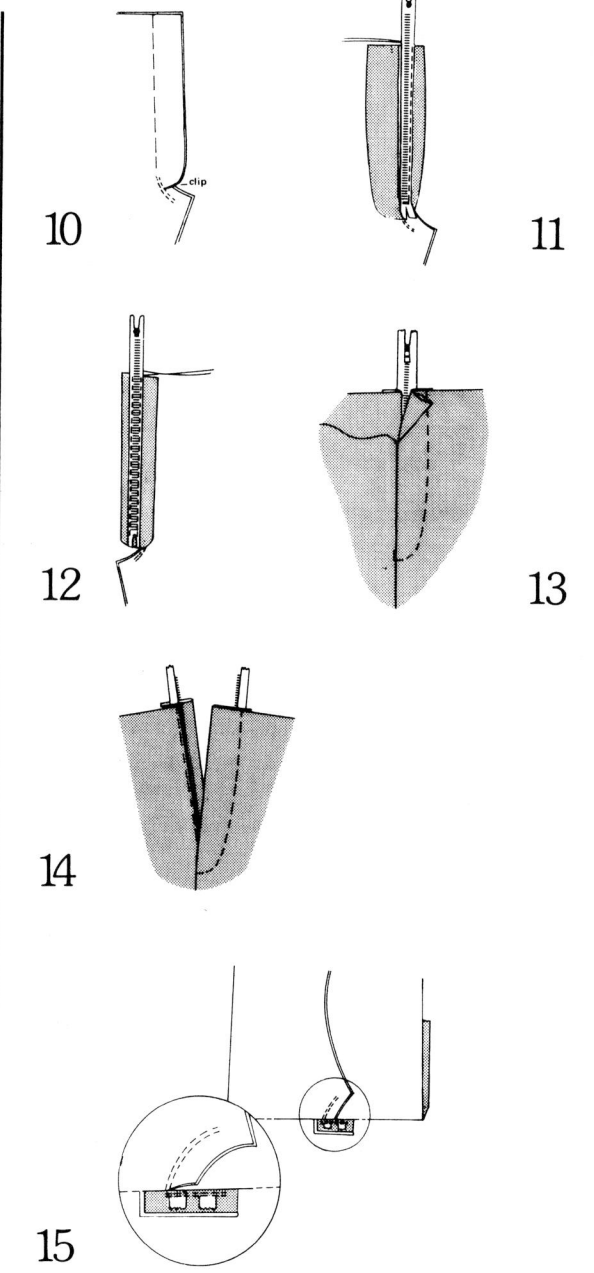

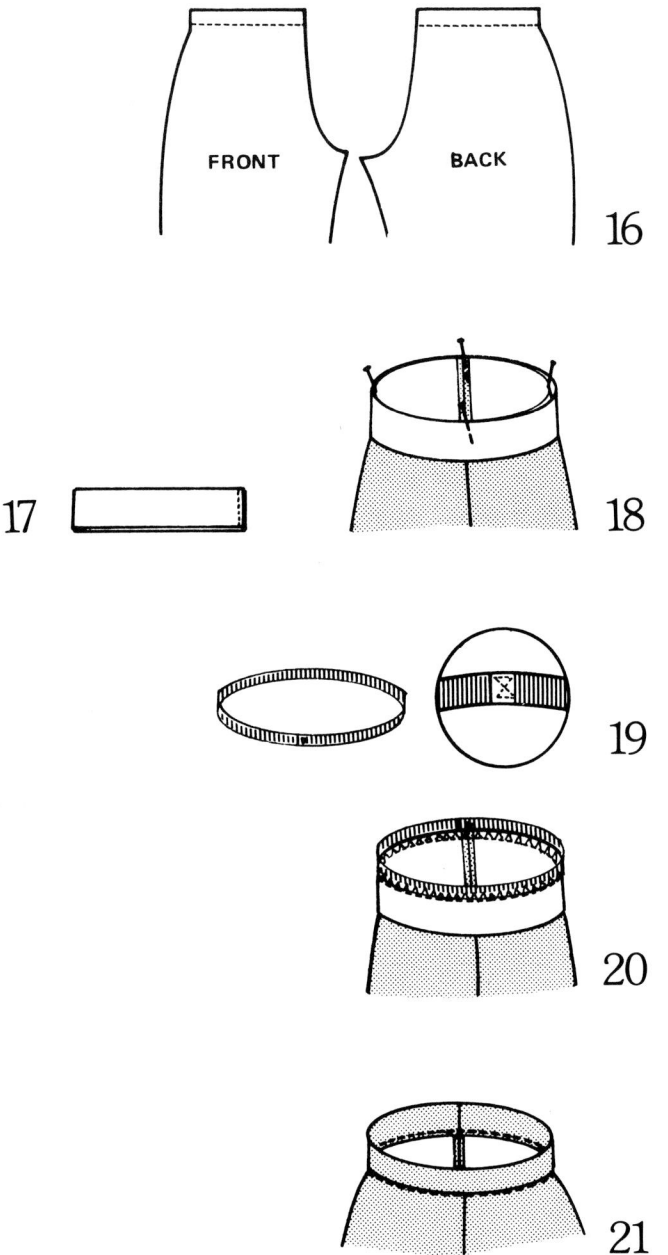

FRONT   BACK

16

17

18

19

20

21

SEPARATE WAISTBAND WITHOUT A CLOSURE

In order to add a waistband without a closure to Pattern 700, you must use fabric with 30 to 50 per cent stretch. Subtract 7/8 inch from the top of the front and back pattern pieces. (Fig. 16) Cut a strip of fabric approximately 3-1/2 inches wide and 2 inches longer than your waist measurement plus 5/8 inch seam allowances. The stretch of the fabric must go the length of the strip.

With right sides together, stitch the short ends of the strip together. (Fig. 17) Divide the waistband casing into four equal parts. Pin it, right sides together, to the pants top, matching the quarter divisions with the four pants seams. (Fig. 18) Stitch with a 5/8 inch seam allowance and stretch hard as you sew.

Cut a piece of Stretch and Sew brand 1-inch waistband elastic as long as your waist measurement plus 1 inch. Lap the cut ends of the elastic 1/2 inch and stitch securely. (Fig. 19) Divide the elastic into 4 equal parts and position it between the seam allowance and the waistband casing, matching the divisions. Pin the elastic in place and stitch it to the seam allowance with a zigzag stitch if available. (Fig. 20) If you use a straight stitch, stretch as you sew the elastic to the seam allowance. Fold the waistband casing firmly over the elastic to the inside of the pants. Pin it in place and stitch-in-the-ditch from the right side. (Fig. 21)

WAISTBAND WITH A CLOSURE

If you have added a fly with a zipper to your pants, you will want a waistband with a closure. Cut a strip of fabric approximately 3-1/2 inches wide and 3-1/2 inches longer than your waist measurement plus two 5/8 inch seam allowances. If a tab extension is preferred, add the desired extra length to the full waistband and elastic measurement. Remember to exclude this extra length when dividing the band in fourths before applying it to the waist of the pants.

Cut a strip of Stretch and Sew 1-inch elastic 1-1/2 inches longer than your body waist measurement. If you would like to use wider elastic, the width of the waistband should be adjusted accordingly. For each 1/2 inch in width of waistband elastic, add 1 inch in width to the waistband piece. As you increase the width of your waistband, check to see if you need additional ease. If your rib section is close to your waistline, your waist size will increase rapidly as you add width to the waistband. For best results, place a piece of elastic the desired width around your waist and check to see if you will need to increase your waist size.

Subtract the seam allowance from each end of the waistband casing and divide the rest into four equal parts. Divide the waist of your pants into four equal parts and match the waistband to the pants, excluding the 5/8 inch seam allowances. Sew with a 5/8 inch seam allowance and stretch as you sew to ease the extra fullness from the pants evenly into the waistband. (Fig. 22) Take special care when stitching over the zipper teeth. Ease the sewing machine needle carefully between the teeth. After stitching, cut the zipper off even with the seam allowance.

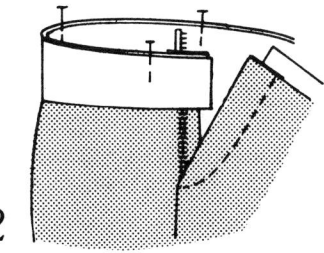

22

Position the elastic between the waistband and the seam allowance. The elastic should be even with the pants at each end so the 5/8 inch seam allowance of the waistband will extend beyond the elastic. Sew the elastic to the seam allowance with a zigzag stitch. (Fig. 23) If you

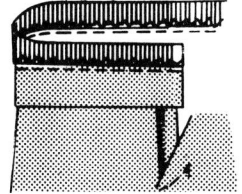

23

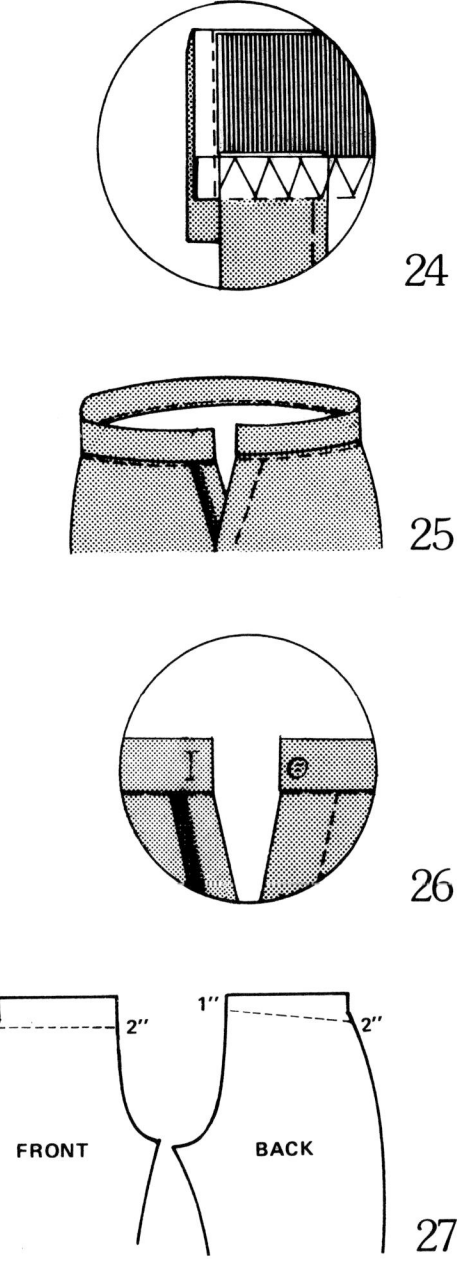

24

25

26

2″ - - - - - 2″   1″ - - - - - 2″

FRONT   BACK

27

have extended the waistband for a tab, the elastic should fill the tab portion up to the seam allowance. Do not stretch the portion of elastic which extends into the waistband tab.

Finish each end by folding the waistband sections lengthwise, right sides together. Stitch across the ends with a 5/8 inch seam. (Fig. 24) Do not catch the elastic into this stitching. Fold the waistband firmly over the elastic to the wrong side. Pin it in place and stitch-in-the-ditch from the right side. (Fig. 25) Sew a hook closure to the end of the waistband. A button may be sewn to the top for a fashion look. (Fig. 26)

HIP HUGGERS

For a hip hugger, drop the waist 2 inches across the front and taper it to a 1-inch drop across the back. The back will fit better if only 1 inch is removed from the top. (Fig. 27) Before you apply elastic to the top of the pants, slip them on to determine if any fullness should be removed from the hip. Because of the difference in the fit of hip huggers, less ease is required.

You may apply regular 3/4 inch elastic by following the technique described in the pattern instructions. To determine the length of your elastic, use a measurement taken from below the waist minus 1 inch instead of your waist measurement minus 1 inch.

The firmer Stretch and Sew waistband elastic also may be used. In this case, use the 1 inch elastic and stitch it to the cut edge of the pants top in the usual manner. Then turn the elastic to the inside and stitch-in-the-ditch on all four seams. This is an especially nice finish when worn with a body suit or blouse.

BELT LOOPS

For a simple belt loop, cut a strip of fabric 1 inch wide. The length should be the width of the waistband plus 1 inch. Fold the strip lengthwise in thirds with the right side out and sew down the center with a small zigzag stitch or two rows of straight stitching. (Fig. 28)

Place the right side of the strip against the inside of the waistband and stitch it across the top. (Fig. 29) Turn the strip to the right side and, folding the raw edge under, stitch it again. This stitching can be on the waistband itself or just below the waistband. (Fig. 30)

Other, more elaborate, belt loops may be made and sewn on in a similar way. (Fig. 31) After drawing a design on your *Perky* Pattern Paper or *Do-Sew*, cut two pieces for each loop and sew them, right sides together, leaving one end free for turning. Turn them to the right side and press them carefully before sewing them to the pants waistband. Often a button replaces the second stitching of the belt loop.

The addition of a fly closure and a waistband will give a totally different look to your garment and yet, imagine, you have done it all yourself, using a simple, basic pattern as your guide. You are well on your way to being the creative person you have always dreamed of being, with the added plus of having a pant wardrobe styled for any occasion.

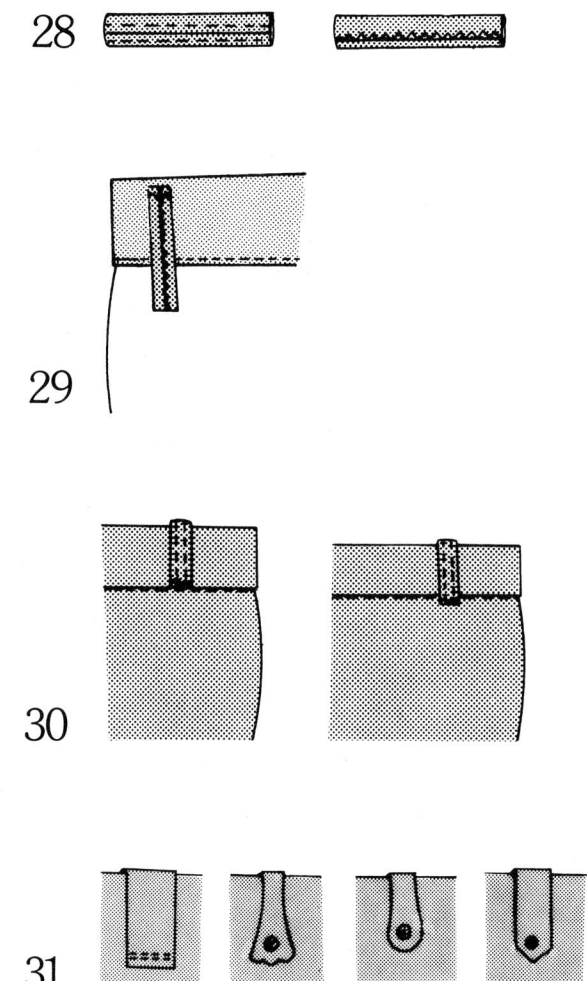

28

29

30

31

Index

A

acrylic, 7
alterations
    crotch depth, 12-13
    hip, 11
    length, 13-14
    special fitting problems, 17-28
        dropped seat, 26
        flat derriere, 18
        flat derriere and flat tummy, 22
        flat side hip, 22
        flat tummy, 21
        heavy upper thigh, 22
        high hip, 26
        large derriere, 18
        large derriere and large tummy, 21-22
        large tummy, 21
        long back, 25
        low hip, 26-28
        short back, 25
        slim upper thigh, 25
        swayback, 25
    waist, 11-12

B

baggies, 38
belt loops, 63
bias, 5-6
blends of fibers, 7
bonding
    Perky Bond, 33-34
    Perky Bond Plus, 46-47, 51-53

C

children's pants, 7
cotton, 7
    double knit, 4, 7
creases
    pressing, 4, 7, 31-34
    twisted, 18, 21-22, 26, 28, 31-32
crotch curve, 17
crotch depth, 12-13, 17
crotch shelf, 17
cuffs
    fake, 40
    for legs flared at seamlines, 41
    for legs flared by slashing and spreading, 41
    for straight legs, 40-41

D

drafting, 37, 48
dry cleaning, 6-7
drying fabric, 6-7

E

ease, 3, 12, 31, 45
elastic, 11-12

F

fabric
    care, 6-7
    creasing properties, 4, 31

T

topstitching, 45-46

V

variations (see style variations)

W

waistband
    belt loops, 63
    hip huggers, 62
    with a closure, 60-62
    without a closure, 60

waist measurement, 11-12
washing fabric, 6-7
wool, 6-7
wrinkles, 7, 17

Y

yokes, 45-46

Z

zipper, 58-59